David L. Hostetler
The Carver

David L. Hostetler
The Carver

Directed and Designed by
Terrill E. Eiler

Essays & Research by
Richard Wootten
Louis Zona, Ph.D.
Barbara Bays, Ph.D.

Picture Research
Lyntha Scott Eiler

Editorial Support
Shelly Bowen
Mark Crosten
Holly Panich
Laura Elliott
Susan Crehan Hostetler

Editorial Board
Kenneth C. Frisch
Holly Panich
Martha Turnage
Terrill E. Eiler
Dora J. Wilson

Ohio University Press
Athens

Copyright

Wooten, Richard
     David L. Hostetler, the carver / Text by Richard Wootten; compiled and edited by Terrill E. Eiler.
          p.   cm.

ISBN 0-8214-1024-5
     1. Hostetler, David L. 2. Sculptors--United States--Biography. 3. Wood-carvers--United States--Biography. I. Eiler, Terrill E. II Title.
NB237.H63W66 1992
730'.92--dc20
{B}
                                                                              91-3689
                                                                              CIP

Contents

Acknowledgements

Starting a project of this scope without a dream is impossible. The dream of this book belongs to Glenn Randall. An unpredictable force of alumni and friends kept Glenn's idea alive. The support of the following people who were part of that force should be recognized. Without the 1804 Fund and Glenn Randall this project could not have started. Without the funding, photographs, and energy provided by these individuals, this book would not have been accomplished. *T. Eiler*

The following provided financial support to underwrite the research and preparation of this project.
Dr. and Mrs. Vernon R. Alden
Mr. and Mrs. James Allen
Mr. and Mrs. Robert Axline
Mr. and Mrs. Rufus C. Barkley, Jr.
Mr. and Mrs. G. Kenner Bush
Cardinal Industries/ David Baker
Dr. Martha L. King
Dr. and Mrs. Wilfred R. Konneker
Drs. Paul and Laura Mesaros
Mr. and Mrs. J. Wallace Phillips
Dr. and Mrs. Charles J. Ping
Mr. and Mrs. Glenn Randall
Mr. and Mrs. Alan Riedel
Mr. Ruben Shohet
Larry and Klara Silverstein
Mr. Milton J. Taylor
The Ohio University 1804 Fund

The work of these talented photographers provided the visual chronicle of David's life and art (Ohio University Degrees & dates in italic).
Yousuf Karsh, *LHD 1965*
Carl Fleischhauer, *MFA 1969*
Jon Webb, *BFA 1966*
Larry Gregory, *MFA 1972*
David Gilmore, *AB 1963, MFA 1969*
Dana Vibberts, *BFA 1954, MFA 1966*
Terrill E. Eiler, *BFA 1966, MFA 1969*
Brian Blauser, *BFA 1965*
Fred Schnell
David Perry
Paul Fusco, *BFA 1957*
Monty Calvert, *1966*
Laura Elliott, *1992*
R. L. Palmer, *BFA 1958, MFA 1960*
Terry S. Lindquist, *MFA 1959*
Bates Littlehales

The assistance and encouragement of these individuals was critical to the publishing of this book.
Jack G. Ellis
Dora J. Wilson
Kenneth C. Frisch
Gretchen Stephens
Beverly Schumacher
Randolph Coleman

Foreword:

by Glenn C. Randall

I met David Hostetler in the early 1950's while I was a first year student and he was a professor at Ohio University. Our paths first crossed outside the classroom at Moe Tritipo's "Trading Post", a frontier-type second–hand store near the university. We both frequented Tritipo's searching for antiques and forms. I had just discovered and purchased from "Ole Moe" a very good early American, colonial period, cherrywood candlestand with graceful spider legs, when David and I met.

Being a Fine Arts major I realized who Professor Hostetler was, because he taught one of my degree requirements — sculpture. I remember this first meeting because Hostetler immediately put me at ease. He demonstrated concern and interest in me while still conveying a strong inner confidence in himself. You trusted and believed David Hostetler. He made you pay attention and listen. His interest and enthusiasm were contagious. We discussed in depth the candlestand and a life-long friendship was established. A lot of "tradin" of goods and sharing of experience have continued down through the years.

This very friendly, jovial, thorough, intelligent and very talented man was indeed an artist of the highest order. I learned he was a teacher of students not just a teacher of subject matter. He often shared and lived the times with his students, to convey his wisdom. He was also hard at work perfecting the skills that make him the single most important living figurative sculptor in America. David Hostetler enjoys a national reputation and has works in numerous important museums and private collections. He has been hard at work sculpting for over forty years. His output is significant. However, he has not been forced to produce for the sake of production. He has not been tainted by commercialization.

Today, as before, David Hostetler is driven by his art. Integrity and passion in his work have a way of coming through the force that drives his gouge. His early sculptures, as well as the more recent creations, at our home at Clarendon Court, are timeless.

This book is the first attempt at putting into perspective David Hostetler's artistic achievements. It will document his position among American sculptors of the 20th century. In the 1990's, I feel that David

Glenn Randall and David Hostetler 1989

Hostetler is really just being discovered. With this publication, he will start to receive the recognition and acclaim that is long overdue. Not only are his curvilinear American women sculptures beautiful and pleasing, they are still available and affordable. •

Artist's Statement:

My life centers around what I call artful choices—choices about life rhythms, shapes, and spaces and their infinite combinations. My lover, my nest, carving on a log, drumming, woodland meditation, archery, whatever, all are involved with these artful choices. At times in my life, this ever-present concern for the forms, shapes, textures, and rhythms of things seems more like a curse than a blessing. But at this time in my life, I can see that anytime I feel centered, serene, in the groove—whatever it may be called—it has had to do with these artful concerns coming together in a subconscious way. This coming together of all the elements is best when it just happens—when the carving, the drumming, the bow and arrow become one with you. In drumming, it is called "finding the groove," when the subconscious takes over.

Having grown up in a rational western culture, it has been very difficult for me to let go of my western rational controlling self and get in touch with the deeper, freer, subconscious images. But, being western, it is more difficult yet to learn to trust these thoughts and images.

I was very fond of my time in the psychedelic sixties. It provided me with the means to shed some of my "brought-up" personal traits with which I had been fighting since childhood and to cultivate my subconscious garden of dream images. It was in the sixties that I first realized how important these images are to my art. Later in the eighties I started drawing these images during the night as they occurred. The semaphore series started as a beautiful vivid dream. I still have to work on trusting these images from my unknown side and as this trust grows so does my art. Now my work is more about my connection to all humans in all times—a group race memory. These images are titled *"ikon"*, *"archetype"*, *"idol."* Before my concerns were for here-and-now images.

I suppose I never had an alternative to a life of woodcarving if you believe in biological destiny. My Swiss, Hochstetler, ancestors were whittlers and carvers in the town of Hochstetler in Canton-Bern. Many of them became the Amish we now know in the mid-west. My son also works in wood.

Art is my life
by David L. Hostetler

The closest I get to the groove, serenity, is when I've been carving for hours and most of this world becomes tuned out. From this I get a fulfillment that gives me sanity. I carved my first wood sculpture in 1957, the year Brancusi died and my son was born. It was in black walnut from my farm on Coolville Ridge. Doing it, I was influenced by Raoul Hague, to whom Jim Dine had introduced me on one of our many New York City art trips. I loved the directness of his carving, and still do. I have played with and lived with wood since my childhood. I am enamored with its feel, its color, its shapeability, but most of all with the fact that it is a living material. It has a life that mirrors our own; it records the seasons; our very existence on this planet is recorded in its calendar of growth rings. When I'm meditating in my woods, I'm literally a tree hugger and often place my ear on a tree to listen to its inner voice, sounds and rhythms. Trying to get in tune with the big rhythms of life might explain my life-long love affair with drums and drumming. The coming together of art, rhythm, forms, and space can be magic. The quest for this magic gives my life purpose and provides for my joy of being.

Art is my life! •

Preface:

As our car approached Coolville Ridge, a hilly area east of the Hocking River in Athens, Ohio, my anticipation of seeing an old friend heightened. He is a man possessed with a remarkable amount of good humor, vitality and personality.

He is David Hostetler, one of America's top figurative sculptors, a unique phenomenon in the world of art, and a fun-loving guy. My wife, Jay, and I have known him for more than 20 years and the longer the time span between our meetings the more catching up there is to do. And catching up on the activities of Hostetler's multi-faceted life can be pretty heady stuff which usually involves a great deal of hilarity.

As the car pulls into the driveway behind his farm house, Hostetler — smiling widely, bearded, tall, gangly — opens his French doors, and approaches with his arms out. In a rich, resonant, baritone voice that has mesmerized his students for forty years, he greets Jay and me with a drawn-out, "Heeeyyy, Jay and Dickie" and a long laugh and bear hugs.

He wants us to see his new studio, his new sculptures, his drawings for other artworks. He has more slides to show. His thousands of students will never forget his slide lectures. They were a laugh a minute. An untiring photographer, he takes pictures of his good times with friends, and he also copies photos of art works that strike his fancy. One wacky unexpected image after another is flashed on the screen, and soon the viewer hurts from too much laughter.

Hostetler has hundreds of friends who range from farmers who live down the road to wealthy chief executive officers of huge corporations who invite him to parties on their yachts.

Two old friends are Yousuf and Estrellita Karsh of Ottawa. Yousuf Karsh, the legendary portrait photographer of such greats as Churchill and Hemingway, photographed Hostetler and his sculptures in Athens in 1967.

Estrellita summed up Hostetler in a phone conversation. She said, "There isn't the slightest bit of guile to David. There's not the slightest edge to him. He is a divine human - funny, witty and a very good friend. He's natural, a complete original, living there in the county on his farm. Ralph Lauren spends half a million to get that effect. David's the kind of man the phonies copy from."

In the 1960s when Hostetler was flirting with the idea of conquering the New York art scene, a psychiatrist familiar with successful New York artists told Hostetler that he smiled too much. "No one will take you seriously if you smile that much," he warned. Hostetler's still smiling.

He backed away from the New York scene, with its intense hype and obligatory role-playing and returned to the farm where he knew who he was. He then proceeded to embark on a series of elegant wood sculptures of women that have made him famous.

His wood sculptures represent the forward edge of an extremely American tradition of solid log carvers that dates back to the bosomy symbolic female figureheads that graced the bows of eighteenth-century sailing ships. Although figureheads had been carved as long ago as Egyptian times, early Americans had refined the art to a high degree of excellence and originality.

And there were the ubiquitous cigar store Indians of the nineteenth century that warm the heart of any lover of American history. They were symbols of commerce, enterprise and the much-sought-after good smoke. And popping up in folk art collections are numerous carvings by anonymous artists who whittled away at the fast disappearing forests as the frontier moved westward.

Hostetler's sculptures - both wood and bronze - continue that rich tradition. Seen in the light of that tradition, his female figures (rather unbosomy landlubbers) whose style, dress and carriage successfully define the essence of American womanhood, serve to make Hostetler perhaps the "most American" figurative carver living today.

Over the years I have frequently watched him work on carvings. He holds a gouge in his hand lightly, as if it were a feather. He will examine a friend's newly-carved picture frame with the same lack of grip. The touch is reverent as if the object held were some delicate fourteenth-century manuscript painstakingly illuminated by a monk.

Hostetler's carving tools are lined up neatly and in order, hanging in racks in his studio. Being born a Capricorn accounts for his sense of order, he says. He sharpens his blades with such expertise that a gouge slices into wood with the slightest pressure.

His devotion to his art is inspirational to fellow artists, students, collectors and other admirers. The publicity he received in the national press in the 1960s helped to put Ohio University on the map. He was "good copy" to editors of newspapers and magazines, including *Time*.

Although Hostetler's own distinctive formal style is semi-abstract, the viewer examining a piece rarely furrows a brow. Angst, an element in so much other contemporary art, isn't present. And if his art is a celebration of women, it is also a celebration of life. His vitality, in both his art and life, is catching. His message is clear: life is fun. And today, he says he has never been happier or freer. Somerset Maugham had it right. The artist is the only free man. Hostetler is that man. •

Personal thoughts
by Richard Wootten

Woman 1948.

Of Growth and Change

Chapter I

Anyone who has known Hostetler over a period of time can't help but feel they have known many Davids. In 1967 he wore an Edwardian black suit to his exhibit in Cleveland. It resembled the type the Beatles wore. He later burned it. In 1968 he sported a black Amish broad-brimmed hat at his farm. Within a few years it was a pigtail and a red `granny rag' on his head.

Always self-effacing, he recalled the time in Nantucket when a photo was being taken of one his reflective chrome busts. The idea was to take the shot so that his reflection and that of the island's historic windmill would be visible on the surface of the shiny sculpture. A small boy wandered by, saw the sculpture and asked what it was. David said it was art. "What's it for?" the youth asked. The youngster never really got an adequate answer.

That is not to say that some of his works have not had utilitarian purposes. Hostetler remembers a time when a woman visited his farm in 1967. A camera crew was busy there photographing his female carving inside a new American Motors car for a television commercial. The woman asked to look at sculptures in his studio. Hostetler recalled with a chuckle,"I tried to tell her they were rather expensive but that she was welcome to look around. I got involved with the camera crew and she came back and said she found one. I told her the price was $1,500 and she said, 'Fine I'll take it.' I couldn't believe it. Then she told the reason for the purchase. She said that every Christmas Eve her husband, a doctor, had a house call. She explained, 'He was always saying how I was a wooden woman in bed, so this Christmas when he comes home he would find a real wooden woman in bed instead of me!' "

That story is not unique. Hostetler remembered a similar one. One of his tall standing wooden women was in the lobby of the plushest motel in Athens, the Ohio University Inn. One night the manager called excitedly to tell him that the sculpture at the inn had been stolen. "I went down there, and by the time I walked in the lobby everybody was laughing. I asked, 'What's so funny, man? I don't think it's funny.' And they said , 'Well, we found it. The maid turned down the bed in one of the rooms and there it was. Some guy took it to bed the night before.' "

And then there was the use a plastic surgeon in Florida made of a Hostetler abstract carving. The year was 1958, and it was the first sculpture he had ever sold. "I asked him why he had bought my piece and he said, `Well, I just redecorated my office and I charge a lot. I want people to know when they come into my office that they are going to pay some money. This piece says you are going to pay some money.' I was shocked. It took me months to get over that."

And then there was the problem at the Carl Solway gallery in Cincinnati. The gallery director angrily phoned Hostetler to report that a wealthy patron who had bought one of his sculptures was furious. The patron had a white rug under the carving and some substance was obviously seeping from the wood on to the rug, staining it.

David drove to Cincinnati, picked up the carving, returned it to his studio, and hollowed out the center of the piece. "The wood didn't seem wet to me, but I carved it out, took it back, and a week later the dealer called again and this time he was really mad. It happened again. So, I went there again, and the patron's chauffeur shows up carrying the carving, which was of a woman in a white dress. I looked at it. The stain on the wood looked yellow. It smelled bad. I said,`Do you guys have a dog?' It hit them all at once, Oh, my God, they have a little dachshund. The patron was so embarrassed. They wanted it painted. I thought it looked nice so I just put a little bleach on it."

Of course, the vast majority of collectors of Hostetler's enjoy the sculpture visually. David enjoys the idea of creating forms that people can idolize. By concentrating on the grace of the female form in his artworks, he believes he is providing art of intrinsic appeal.

In one of his carefully composed artist's statements written for a 1968 Boston exhibition,he expressed it this way:

"My sculpture is woman with the mark of the present and the past cultures on her. Timeless woman as an object, a goddess, angular, sensual, stylized; but always filled with grace and vitality that is woman. Woman to me is the ideal form, erotic yet pure, compositionally variable, yet identical every time.

"My medium is wood, the American elm that grows on and around the farm where I live. Wood appeals to my close affinity with nature and things organic. Wood is a magic material, alive and working, organic, and never completely at rest. I am concerned with the integration of a selected wood's grain with the carved form of my sculpture. Our ephemeral existence is recorded in these same grain rings."

Since making that statement, his choices of materials have undergone a change. One patron has made a point of supplying him with more exotic woods with interesting grain patterns.

He also is doing more bronze figures. The first bronze was a sort of experiment. When Vernon Alden was president of Ohio University in the 1960s, he wanted a piece for his garden. Since wood is not an outdoor material, one of Hostetler's students who was working in the foundry suggested that they try casting a wooden piece in bronze. An attempt was made and it was successful.

Since then, many such transferences have been made; however, wood pieces whose beauty depend a great deal on the appeal of the wood and grain are not cast.

The Swiss sculptor Alberto Giacometti, one of Hostetler's favorite sculptors, once said that it was by means of style that works of art attain truth. Hostetler's distinctive and unique style has been established firmly since the late 1960s. The truth Hostetler seeks is the essence of form, with woman as the subject.

Siren 1957.

Before that, however, he experimented in styles by studying the works of established sculptors and other cultures. There was an Archipenko-like glazed clay figure from 1952; an Easter Island totem-like Sculp-Metal piece in 1954; a thin, kneeling Giacomettiesque piece in plaster from 1955; a Raoul Hague-like torso (his first wood figure) in 1957; some Lachaise-like, ample-bosomed torsos in 1958; and, during the same year, a seated woman in bronze inspired by Henry Moore.

Before embarking on folk-oriented figures in the early 1960s, he created two extremely sexy and anatomically realistic bikini-clad carvings in the late 1950s.

Then he went for a year and a half without carving anything. He started his farm on Coolville ridge. Without the use of farm machines, he, his wife and children and students did the haying by hand and took care of 170 chickens, goats (Nubians), and 13 Herefords. He helped the neighboring farmers bring in the crops. He was finding his roots by living a pre-industrial revolution simple life similar to that of his Amish ancestors.

From that began the Amish figures that by the mid-1960s were metamorphosing into slim, fashion forms.

Looking back over forty years of modeling and carving sculptures, Hostetler views the development of his style as cyclical, not linear. "I keep cycling. I will work on a piece in which texture is important. Then I'll do a piece in which smoothness is important," he said.

"Two early pieces demonstrate what I've been into all along. There is a 1946 seated nude done naturalistically and a 1947 seated nude done abstractly. They prove that I've been interested in naturalization and formalization all along. The two approaches are a constant with me.

"I'm getting more textural now in my pieces but it's not the first time. At one time I worked with a hatchet and went back years later to smooth them all out. So I deflect between rough and smooth. But taken as a whole, I'd say my style is more formal than natural. The gluteus maximus on a 1953 female figure is the same as in 1989. The shape of the breasts in 1961 are not that far from what I've done in 1989.

"Even my early 1961 *Gotham Girl* is built up of formal shapes - it's not loosey goosey and neither am I. I may have given the appearance in my alcohol-laden days in the 1970s of being a lot looser than I really was. As a psychologist friend of mine told me, 'David, you're really an introvert.' That's why I put a quote up on the wall of my studio that says, 'By the time I found out I was an introvert, I was too old to do anything about it.'"

Hostetler has also stretched out his figures to unnatural heights at various times. He did tall, thin Giacometti-like clay forms in the mid-fifties and elongated wood pieces from time to time in the seventies and eighties.

Hostetler is the first to point out that the only time his female forms seem extremely distorted - thin heads, curvaceous swan necks - is when he has gone through some emotional trauma, such as his break-ups with wives and lovers. One piece, a fragmented torso in bronze done at the time of his first divorce in 1970, finally outstayed its welcome in exhibitions and was melted down.

Do Hostetler's female forms represent specific women? He routinely refuses to do commissions, he says, because "it is nearly impossible to match someone else's dreams and images with your own desires and forms."

Since the faces of his figures are abstract suggestions of facial features, none of his works could be called portraits. However, he has

Photograph by Terry E. Eiler

The Bather 1961.

incorporated hairdos, dresses and shapes of actual people in his work.

They range from early carvings representing his two daughters, his first wife, June (a seated figure), his companion Doni Grix of the mid-1970s (*Dancing Woman*), his friend Lisa Eckerle of the early 1980s (hands lifting hair in suggestive dance pose) and his wife Susan Crehan (*Deco Lady*). And during the 1960s he created several works inspired by Marion Alden, wife of Ohio University President Vernon Alden.

Generally, his female sculptures exude a light-hearted self-assurance. If they could speak they might say, "Yes, I am certain of my self and my beauty."

Since retiring in 1985 as a full professor of sculpture from Ohio University, where he had taught since 1948 and where he was named a University Professor in 1979, he is enjoying the pleasures of a successful career of a full-time artist.

He and Susan live on the farm from fall through spring and spend the summers in Nantucket where they have a second home and run their own gallery.

A new studio graces the 40-acre farm in Athens, where Hostetler creates his latest masterpiece, a large amorphous bronze with an elongated hole in the middle. The opening is the outline of a life-size female form. Perhaps it will be placed at a specific spot on the farm so that on the first day of spring the sun would shine through it to another reflective sculpture. If so, it would be a good excuse for a celebration and drumming.

Better a Chicken on your Lap than a Father on your Neck

The old man held a chicken on his lap and was talking to it. The young boy stood beside them and entered the conversation. The year was 1931 and the place was Beach City, Ohio, a tiny rural town near Massillon.

Today, David Hostetler can't recall what he and his grandfather said to that chicken, but he does remember the good times he and Grandpa George Penrod had going fishing together, digging up rutabagas in the winter and collecting eggs from the chicken house. He knows that there was something "real" and "connected" about his mother's father that has had a deep influence on his own life.

Was it that George Penrod was a carpenter by trade? Or was it the sense of adventure that his grandfather embodied? "I remember he kept a 'peacemaker' under his pillow," recalled Hostetler. "He'd bring out the gun and tell me about the West, about punching cattle. He'd have a hole in his pants and he'd say he got the hole the day that he didn't have time to draw. He just shot the guy right through his own pants. Was he really Out West? Who knows?"

The answer too may have been that Grandpa George was a great fantasizer, aided and abetted by his standing in the family as a "fine old hard drinkin' gent."

David Hostetler was born in that little town of Beach City on December 27, 1926. As he put it, on a PBS documentary, "I simmered up in Beach City, Ohio, and where there's no beach and no city. There's hardly anything there. It's a very rural place."

Except for a print of Gainsborough's *Blue Boy* that his father's mother had, the young David was never exposed to art. He says there was never anything at home that could have possibly directed him into art.

But fantasy abounded in the imagination of this skinny only child of Melwood and Grace Penrod Hostetler, especially when visiting Grandpa George's village farm and also the farm of his other grandfather

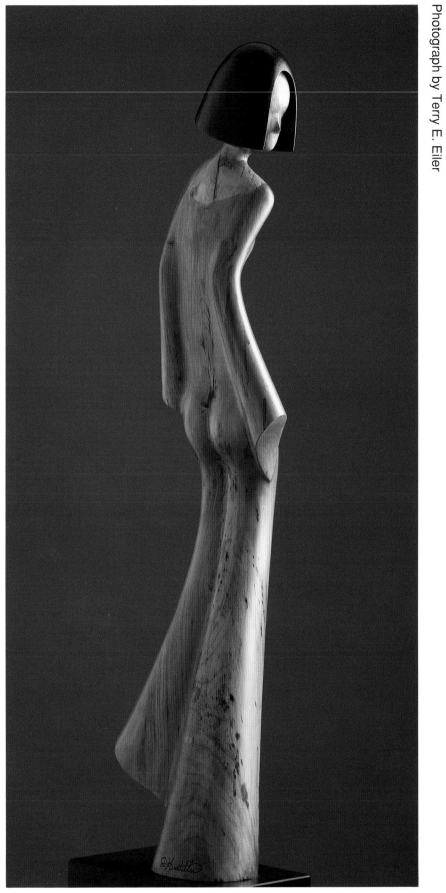

Summertime Lady 1977.

in Greenville, Ohio, "where I would climb water windmills and pretend that they were whatever I wanted them to be.

"Being an only child, I created a lot of fantasy," he recalled, "I remember making dioramas in my room. I used paraffin for ice. Outside in Greenville I'd make whole little villages around a tree. I'd have tin soldiers in caves, and cut up tin cans to make airplane hangers. They were always three dimensional. I was replicating —making my own life. And now, after all of these years, I think more and more that creating art is a matter of creating your own life."

Hostetler realized in later life that he had always seen things three-dimensionally, in layers of planes. He hadn't thought of this vision as a gift — as some people have perfect pitch or a photographic memory — until he learned that many other people view things frontally. Obviously, this gift has played a major role in his shaping of forms.

Hostetler also has a hunch that his woodcarving obsession may be firmly implanted in his chromosomes. In doing some research on his father's side of the family, he found that the Hochstetlers in Switzerland are all carvers. While Grandpa George was an amiable character, his other grandfather scared him.

"My father's father, Bowman Hostetler, was a hellfire fundamentalist minister, a First Christian traveling in tent shows. My father grew up moving with him from town to town and attending twenty-two different Ohio schools," he recalled.

"I spent the summers in Greenville while my father went to college. It took him years to get a degree. He didn't start until he was twenty-eight. I slept in a bedroom over Grandpa Hostetler's library and I'd hear a lot of shouting. I'd hear him revving up for his sermons . He frightened the hell out of me. He'd scream things like `Patience, boy!' He was not exactly humorless, but certainly not a man given to joking."

Bowman Hostetler had broken away from his Amish roots and his son, Melwood (David's father), echoed the minister's criticisms of the Amish during David's childhood. As David noted, "Those that leave the Amish farm go either into teaching or the church. They seem to want to cover up their Amish roots." Years later, David's fascination with the Amish was to surface in his sculpture.

Melwood Hostetler was a teacher in Beach City and later was to become principal of a junior high school in Massillon. A World War I veteran who served in the Army as a truck driver, he seemed happiest when attending American Legion meetings. A frustrated entertainer, he loved playing the piano; his letters home during the war were filled with requests for new ragtime war tunes. When he drove his truck close to the battlefields, he referred to the front as the "big music." He was bitterly disappointed when he failed to be transferred to an army vaudeville unit that entertained the troops.

David recalled: "In Massillon he was the commander of the American Legion. He and his veteran friends went back to France, which was the high point of his life. He was made an honorary citizen of Le Mans, France. The army experience for many is the only time a person really lives and is free. For me it was the most hideous part of my life."

In Massillon, where Mel and Grace Hostetler and their son had moved in 1931, David was to grow up feeling left out of the kind of good times his father shared with his doughboy buddies.

He said, " My father seemed guilt-ridden because of the duty he felt that he owed his family. He was a chronic letter writer who would quote Emerson and his `duty calls' message. He was very driven,

Dancer 1975.

neurotic, harsh — and sometimes a bully, really. He was born a patriot. He had dutifully helped raise his brother and sister. Somehow his parents molded him into a very obsequious person. His mother, a member of the WCTU was into a lot of repressing. She would grill me about whether my father was drinking or smoking.

"One of the sorrows of my life is that I was never able to talk to my father. Even today if there were some AT&T connection to the beyond, I'd probably not be able to talk to him. With my father and me, I dialed all sorts of numbers but none of them made connections."

During David's youth, he often sided with his mother against his father. "My mother would belittle him behind his back to me because he was so churchy. I would play possum on Sunday, and she'd say I was sick and I couldn't go to church. And we'd wink at each other."

It irked David that his father did not like Grandfather George. "My father couldn't stand our Sunday visits to Grandpa George's house. To him, George wasn't learned. He didn't 'aspire.' Yet to her death, my mother felt she was lucky to have lived with my father. He made her take English lessons so that she would make a better appearance. He was very appearance–conscious. He would drive to Canton to buy a six-pack of beer and come home and pull down the shades to drink it.

"It would also bother him that I would associate with the sons of doctors whose homes he was not invited to. In Massillon, being a school principal was socially zero. Football was everything. And socially, being the football coach was everything. Paul Brown was God."

Brown, who later founded the Cleveland Browns and managed and owned the Cincinnati Bengals, had received his master's degree at Ohio State at the same time as Mel.

David recalled, "I remember Paul Brown coming to our house in Massillon. I'd be out in the field with a football, all 50 pounds of me. Brown said I looked like a colt. He said, 'It's hard to say what will happen when David fills out.' I never did."

Massillon High School's extracurricular activities emphasized football, band, and choir. David does not recall the subject of art being pushed. However, he did begin to get a reputation as being good with scissors. "I was called on to make the posters. I remember a fullback of the Massillon Tigers saying I was the best cutter he'd ever seen."

But as some ministers' sons become hellions, the principal's son, too, was growing rebellious. "I hated authority and my father represented the utmost authority. So I rebelled against him and school, which he represented. I was probably unconsciously trying to embarrass him. I remember being thrown out of English class because I refused to memorize and recite Thanatopsis. I ended up taking shop classes at night and that was an embarrassment to my father. And I loved shop. I was finally making things. I was knurling steel and I'd never done that. In chemistry they let me pass because I built a press in shop class with which I could make an early plastic from formaldehyde. I made Bakelite forms for the class. I still have one."

David's cousin, Ella May Wehl, who is one year David's senior, remembers Mel Hostetler as a moody man and his wife as being "kind of quiet" "At times David's father wouldn't talk," Mrs. Wehl recalled.

David's high school buddy, Tim Milligan, now an antique and art dealer in Evanston, Ill., remembers Mel Hostetler as principal of Longfellow Junior High School, which he attended. David attended Loren Andrews Junior High across town.

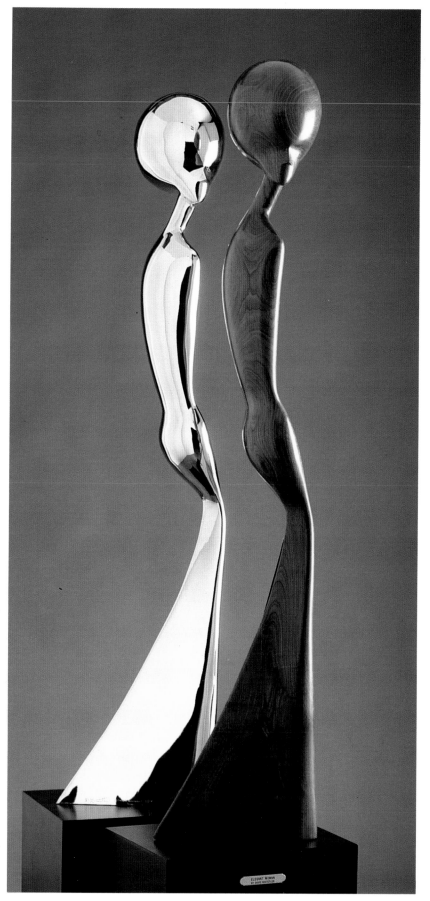

Elegant Woman 1981.

Recalled Milligan, "I remember Mr. Hostetler as a disciplinarian with a heart, an awkward fellow, but a pretty nice, fair fellow. He was tall, angular and bald and combed the hair he had right over the top of his head. He had a mechanical way of playing the piano.

"I remember David playing a kind of primitive boogie-woogie on the piano at the time. He later took up drums. He and I were buddies from the 10th through the 12th grade. We made each other laugh a lot. We came up with a mythical character we called Harvey Alkschmeer and worked a lot of gags with old Harvey. We emblazoned his name on dirty walls in study hall and almost got in a lot of trouble. Harvey's name would pop up in the school annual and newspaper. David loved the scam and he was good at keeping it going.

"He referred to his father as 'Old Mel.' His father was also called Zeke, perhaps because news of his Amish ancestry had leaked out, or maybe because of his Biblical look, and David was called by some people Young Zeke.

"David was extremely popular, personable, and had a very good singing voice, which he used in the choir's bass section. He was pretty good with the girls — not an all-out lady killer — but they liked him. We used to double date a lot. I would be in the back seat with my date and those animals would be in the front seat steaming up the windows.

"After seeing the girls home, we would stand out in front of my house until 5 A.M., philosophizing. He has a good breezy way of talking and keeping everything light with a lot of chuckles. A few years later, after the war, it really surprised me that he wanted to go into art. It flabbergasted me."

Barely eking his way through high school, David saw a way out of his frustrating life. Upon graduation in June 1944, the month American troops landed on D-Day, David enlisted. He was assigned to join the Army Specialized Training Program at Ohio University in Athens in July, to become an army engineer. To his surprise, he found he liked studying calculus. He was among about two hundred recruits planning to become engineering lieutenants who crammed night and day at Scott Quad, the brick dormitory built in 1936 and the university's newest. Marching drills were held in the small yard in the center of the quad. In a recent visit to the quad, David couldn't believe that they marched in such a small area.

He accumulated fifty-four hours towards a college engineering degree in a three-month period. But like everything else in army life, change is the only reliable constant. Change orders abounded and when American troops were suddenly taking a beating at the Battle of the Bulge in December 1944, David and the other would-be engineers traded their slide rules for rifles.

First stop was Camp Atterbury, Indiana, a cold, bleak, flat, harsh place for winter training. There David would sneak out barrack's windows after roll call to get out of detail duty. "My army career was going AWOL and trying to find ways to get out of doing things," he said.

At Camp Fannin, Texas, in a crash course in basic training, he would attend propaganda movies teaching soldiers how to properly hate the enemy.

"We'd come out of the movies screaming 'Kill, Kill, Kill!' and take our bayonets to those dummies. I vacillated between going along with it and fighting it. It was obvious that I was not infantry caliber. I probably weighed 130 pounds. In a big burst of energy, however, I decided to become an expert infantryman and I got all of those shooting medals. The officers in charge wanted to put me in artillery because of my size, but my friends were in the infantry, and although now it seem incredibly foolish, I stayed in the infantry and was sent to the West Coast, probably to be shipped out to Iwo Jima."

An Artistic Recuperation from a California War Wound

It was a fateful incident at San Luis Obispo, California, that pointed the lanky, emaciated eighteen-year-old Ohio rebel in the direction of art. The incident was an accident. While taking part in a training exercise in which soldiers poured from a Higgins boat onto the beach, a simulated shell, usually harmless and designed to give a training session a semblance of realism, went off. Shrapnel was blown into David's leg.

"It probably wouldn't have bothered a lot of people but I was a pretty fatigued kid. My knee got infected. It got worse and worse. Finally, I couldn't walk. The infection had spread to my lymph nodes. So my equipment, including my Brownie camera, was down at the dock in my duffel bag and I was in the hospital. My infantry unit shipped out, along with my duffel bag, and I never saw any of those guys, or my bag, again."

The invalid was transferred to Baker's Field in Pittsburgh, California, to an army hospital where penicillin, then an experimental drug, was injected directly into the lesions of his leg. For six months he was hospitalized. At one point, the staff told him he looked like a victim from Dachau.

It was during this period of recuperation that Hostetler first really became interested in art. He recounted this story to Philip D. Adams, an English professor at Western Michigan University, whose article on Hostetler was printed by the university's school of graduate studies in 1967.

Hostetler told Adams, "The Red Cross used to come around and pass out goodies - food and art. . . . And the guy who was in the bed next to mine took some water colors . . . . He was from Canada, a painter, I guess, a lousy one as I remember . . . . At any rate, he was a painter. And he'd lie there, you know, doing those things, and there wasn't anything for me to do. So the next time that little lady came around, why I took some too. I started drawing, and then we got a couple of guys who could move around in the ward, and we'd get them to stand out there and we'd draw them . Those were the first drawings I ever did, the first art of any sort. . . . And I really dug it, really got turned on, and did some very lousy things which I've since destroyed."

When the invalid could finally walk, he would visit the post library. His mind was taking an intellectual bent by then and he discovered volumes of Shakespeare. He began reading and memorizing the bard. In the library he also met a girl, also about nineteen, who was a college student in Stockton, Calif.

"I was doing a lot of what I called art — water colors — for her. Really, the only thing I was doing was evading the army and pretending I was also into art. But I was wildly in love with her. I would go AWOL to San Francisco to meet her under the clock at the Mark Hopkins Hotel. We wanted to do everything romantically. There was a Judy Garland movie out then about a soldier meeting his girl under a clock - and to us, that was romantic."

Why he wasn't put in the stockade for his persistent AWOLs, David has never really figured out. " I remember hitch-hiking back to the post one time at 4 A.M. and an officer gave me a ride. He told the guard at the gate that I was his guest and we went right through. VJ Day had come and gone, the war was over and things weren't hectic."

A Father's Blunder Spawns a Son's Career

The gimpy hero returned to Massillon in January 1946, ready to take full advantage of his membership in the 52-20 Club. Ex-GI's got twenty dollars a week for fifty-two weeks for rehabilitation. What followed was months of hanging out in bars until 2 or 3 A.M. and sleeping through the days.

But his interest in art had stuck with him. His buddy from high school, Tim Milligan, was attending the Cleveland School of Art with an eye to becoming a commercial artist. Milligan studied with such established painters of the Cleveland School as Carl Gaertener and Frank Wilcox. David even sneaked into some of the classes Milligan was taking. With the vast number of post-war students, instructors didn't notice new faces in the classroom. Tim and David drew together and took part in "hellacious and sophomoric" arguments about the virtues of modern art. David defended Kandinsky abstracts and Tim said they were worthless.

Another artistic influence on David at the time was Albert Hise, the director at the Massillon Museum, and Helen Henley who taught classes in art there. David attended.

Meanwhile, Mel was disturbed at seeing his son go to waste and urged him to continue the engineering studies he had begun in the army. What followed was a father's blunder that resulted in an art — not engineering — education for his son.

Knowing that Purdue University had a renowned engineering school, Mel wrote a letter of application on David's behalf to the Director of Admissions. Purdue was safe in Mel's mind. It didn't have an art department. By mistake he addressed the letter to "Purdue University, Bloomington, Indiana." It was received by the Director of Admissions at Indiana University at Bloomington. David was accepted.

David took his first classes in the summer of 1946 and they weren't engineering classes. He studied art history with Otto Brendel, an art scholar from Columbia University and Germany, and the older man took a liking to the lanky nineteen-year-old.

Something else David learned that summer was that alcohol is a great common denominator. "Anybody can talk to anybody with alcohol, even a sophomoric kid to someone learned," he noted.

"I remember my first argument at art gatherings pitted the fans of naturalism of the North against the believers of the anti-naturalistic, fantasy, Renaissance painters of the South. I remember ranting at parties, defending the northern painters because their art was more 'real' and somehow hit my bucolic background. It was the Southern Titians, Tintorettos versus Brueghel's belching, hiccoughing, peasants of the north, frolicking about with bulging codpieces. That was the first dichotomy in art that engaged me."

David proved himself a dedicated student at Indiana. While other students pursued their social life by joining fraternities and sororities, having dates and getting pinned, David was holding all-nighters painting in a studio. He said he worked so steadily that at one time his hands became nearly paralyzed. "As in the army, I was pushing this body towards some kind of Calvinist penance," he said.

He may also have been following the example of one of his teachers who labored into the wee hours over his canvases. He was a dwarf named Ballinger "who thought he was Toulouse-Lautrec."

Alton Pickins, an art professor and painter who had been pictured in Life magazine in 1946 as one of the ten new "hot" American painters, befriended David.

"I remember him coming in the studio one day, looking around at the other students and telling me, `Hostetler, look at those healthy flowers over there, I expect nothing from them. From you I expect great things, Hostetler, because you are really screwed up."

Another time David had spent all night painting a realistic life-size Jesus figure complete with highlighted tears; and Pickins arrived at 8 A.M. to critique the work.

"I expected praise and admiration from my mentor," said David, "but instead he said, `Hostetler, you've got great technique, but you've got shit for taste in subject matter.'

Again during a painting class I cited something from *Time* magazine and he said, `Hostetler, you always have the most wonderful scholastic sources for your insights.' That really burned. Needless to say, we had a love-hate relationship."

David, stimulated by the heady intellectual atmosphere, found himself drawn to one subject after another. He roomed with a houseful of German Turnverein students ("all built like Rambo who played Wagner on the phonograph and danced wild waltzes") and he tried to learn German.

He was invited to parties at the home of Henry Hope, the head of the art department who collected works for the Museum of Modern Art. His house was filled with Rattners, Shahns, Marinis and Moores. David told him he had decided to become an art historian, but Hope shot down the idea. "You don't have the head for it. You don't know the language," he said. That didn't stop David from taking thirty hours of art history.

At Indiana University he met a Nobel prize winner, a fruit fly researcher named Mueller; B.F. Skinner, the behaviorist; and Kellogg, the educator who had a son raised with an ape. David studied education, psychology, painting, pottery-making and was even interviewed by Kinsey about sex.

He also remembers Gene Johnson, a physicist, who was studying the theory of cold light by examining lightning bugs in jars. They still correspond at Christmas.

David's ideas about becoming a painter changed when he met potter Karl Martz, a gentle person whose wizardry at the potter's wheel fascinated the young student. But by his senior year another art form, sculpture, was to share his interest.

Laurent and Nadelman

Sculptor Robert Laurent (1890–1970) taught sculpture at Indiana University from 1942 to 1961 after having received praise in New York art circles. Born in Brittany, France, he studied drawing and woodcarving in Rome before permanently settling in the United States in 1910. He was influenced by sculpture he saw at the famous 1913 Armory Show and within a few decades was considered a pioneer in Modern Art in America.

Laurent's now-cloying Art Deco style was popular in New York in the 1920s and 1930s and also quite visible to the general public. His aluminum *Goose Girl*, placed in the mezzanine of Radio City Music Hall in 1932, created a stir among the more prudish citizens and was removed. His stylized nudes dominated the New York World's Fair of 1939.

His early figure sculptures were noted for their mannered style, rounded and smoothly flowing surface planes, and elegant, sinuous contour lines. He was praised upon his retirement at Indiana University in 1961 as one of America's most distinguished sculptors, a respected artist and teacher who was known for his sophisticated hospitality.

The catalogue of his 1961 retrospective at Indiana included this telling statement about his reputation: "At Indiana University he continued to win prizes and regain in regional fame at least a part of what he lost by being absent from New York."

When twenty-one-year-old David Hostetler spent his senior year studying sculpture with fifty-eight-year-old Laurent, he felt honored if the master even acknowledged his physical presence in class.

David recalled, "Laurent was the last of the atelier masters. He was of the old school, the last of the dinosaurs. He didn't get into big existential raps. He quietly watched the students and would make an occasional comment. You felt lucky if you got to sharpen his carving tools. And if he spoke to you, you felt rewarded.

"I do remember working on a large figure that I signed boldly in the base with huge letters. He told me that 'perhaps a more modest signature might be appropriate.' I hung around him and spent the summer there watching him."

Fourteen years later, when David had an exhibition of his wood sculptures at the Miami (Florida) Museum of Modern Art, Bernard Davis, who had purchased the works, noted in the exhibition notes that although Hostetler's had studied with Laurent, his work "does not show any resemblance to his tutor's."

However, today, a Hostetler female figure does share some characteristics of a Laurent. The "rounded and smoothly-flowing surface planes and elegant, sinuous contour lines," described in the 1961 catalogue on Laurent, apply to both.

It was Laurent who introduced Hostetler to the sculptures of Elie Nadelman. After watching Laurent work on multiple figures in limestone, David wanted his own first piece to be figures of a couple dancing. Laurent showed him a photograph of Elie Nadelman's *Tango*, and David patterned his carving on it.

(On Dec. 5, 1987 Nadelman's 1919 *Tango* sold for $2.8 million at a Christie's auction. That was the highest price ever paid for an American sculpture.)

Despite his many art classes, David concluded his studies at Indiana University in 1948 with a Bachelor of Arts in Education. Mel Hostetler was somewhat pleased. ●

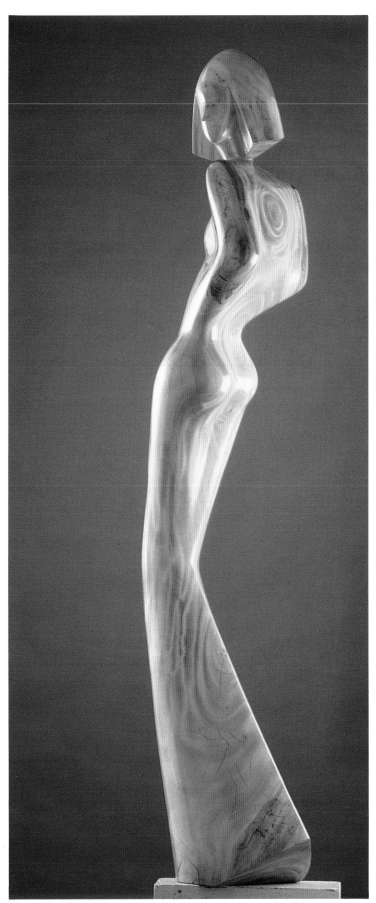

Photograph by Terry E. Eiler

Senuous Woman 1990.

Enju 1948.

Artist and Mentor

Chapter II

Despite the strong impression Laurent made on the fledgling sculptor, the spell that potter Karl Martz cast was even more binding.

David reminisced, "To me what Martz did was like Midas. His folk orientation, simplicity, the idea of taking something worthless like soil, clay and mud and transforming it into something of beauty and value — that had me. He would be lecturing to you and he'd get so quiet you'd have to say 'I can't hear you.' It was almost Oriental the way he taught."

At Indiana University Hostetler was already getting a reputation as an innovative teacher. He and another student instructor would script out lesson plans and present classes as a kind of entertaining theater. "I just had to do something to liven up the classes," he said, "otherwise I would be like some fossilized old educator."

With his mind set on earning a master of fine arts degree, he applied to both Ohio University and Cornell and was accepted at both. He returned to Athens as a graduate assistant in ceramics with a determination to own his own pottery shop. He received his BFA in 1949.

With marriage and the need for a good-paying job on his mind, he tried his hand at commercial art in Canton. He got the job because the employer's astrological charts favored him over other applicants. He soon realized that commercial art was not his thing. A fellow artist at the company told him he lettered like he had a wet banana in his hand.

Although the job paid well he was dissatisfied. He learned about an opening in the Ohio University ceramics department, snapped it up, and spent the next thirty-three years in Athens teaching.

He and his wife, the former June Patterson, whom he had met in Massillon, were soon busy raising a family. David's ceramics studio in the basement of Ellis Hall became so crowded with pottery that the classics professors who taught upstairs began taking offense to it. They called it an apothecary shop. The administration decided he had to move. He bought a pottery studio in town on Highland Avenue. It wasn't long before he had six employees and a booming business.

A brochure from that period included photos of some of the ceramic items for sale. His *Taffeti* decorations on vases, beer mugs,

Figure Model 1945.

Coolville Ridge Studio #1. Background drawing done by Jim Dine.

teapots and plates seem inspired by Jackson Pollock. Continuous thin, free form lines looping about the surfaces constituted the decoration. They were just the thing to go with Danish Modern furniture. Today they seem dated.

Two visitors to his shop made him realize that he really wasn't doing what he wanted to do. One was a representative from a knickknack firm who asked him to produce several hundred salt and pepper shakers in the shapes of outhouses. When he refused, saying he found the idea aesthetically offensive, the visitor pointed out that aesthetics has nothing to do with business. David had to agree.

Claude Renoir, the film director, son of painter Claude Renoir and then a visiting lecturer at Ohio University, stopped by the shop one day. He and David had a long friendly chat about mass producing art. Renoir said it was impossible to produce real art in mass. He also said that being a nineteenth-rate sculptor was better than being a first-rate potter. David wasn't convinced at the time but the thought began eating at him.

Soon David began to concentrate on making single, life-sized ceramic figures in bright colors. They were Giacometti-like, skinny and grotesque. The eyebrows of his business partner, Hunter Hooe, a retired engineer, were raised. He said such behavior was something someone did in retirement years.

"For someone as anti-authoritarian as I was, that was like pouring turpentine in a raw wound," David said. "I decided that then was the time to make sculpture. So I offered to sell him my part of the business. He bought it and I bought a farm on Coolville Ridge east of town."

Purchased in 1955, the farm, where Hostetler still lives, has taken on a vital role in his life. It has become his home base, a refuge, retreat, his "Thoreauesque Eden, Arcadia, blissful utopian place." It has also been the site of numerous parties, bluegrass music-making sessions, and intellectual gab fests. Artists, collectors, curators, photographers, advertising executives and students by the hundreds have visited the farm to enjoy David's irrepressibly cheerful company.

The corn crib, which he converted into a carver's studio, was soon too small. With the help of students, he built a larger studio complete with fireplace, office, cabinets, workbench, racks of gouges and rocking chairs.

The woods on the forty-acre farm were filled with elm trees, sadly stricken with Dutch Elm disease. In 1957 David carved his first wooden sculpture from one of them. But by then, a new important influence had entered his life in the person of a young student - Jim Dine. •

Hostetler and Ralph Hurst at Indiana University, 1947.

Sally Hope, David, and Robert Laurent, 1947

Jim Austin, Cliff Wood, Hostetler at Athens farm, 1950s.

Photograph by Merritt C. Flom

The Tango 1948.

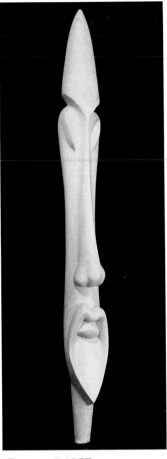

Hostetler 1949.

"Persona" 1957.

Lawrence "Pappy" Mitchell and Hostetler in Ellis Hall ceramic classroom, 1952.

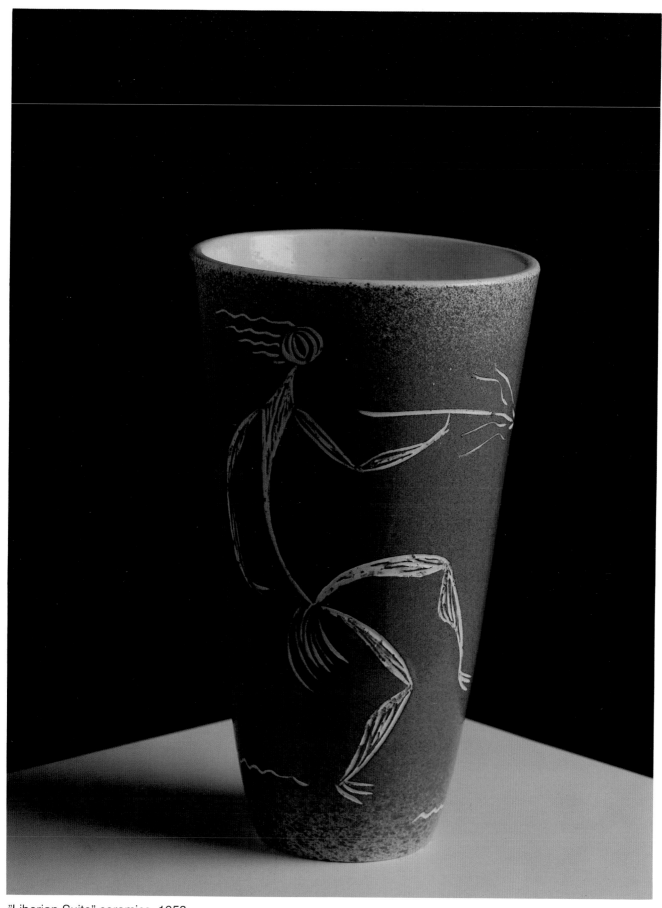

"Liberian Suite" ceramics, 1953.

Reclining Woman 1958.

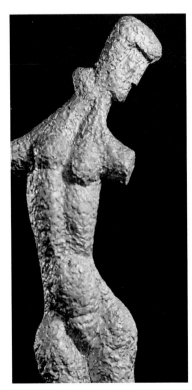

Woman 1948.

Standing Woman 1958.

Nude Torso 1948.

Hostetler pottery, 1950/1955.

Hostetler pottery caricature mug.

Hostetler, ceramic instructor, 1950/1955.

Crucifix 1956.

San Miguel, 1958.

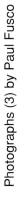

Crucifix 1956.

Stilt Man #1 1955.

Photograph by R. L. Palmer

Holding *Pater Familias* 1954; Coolville Ridge Studio #1, 1958.

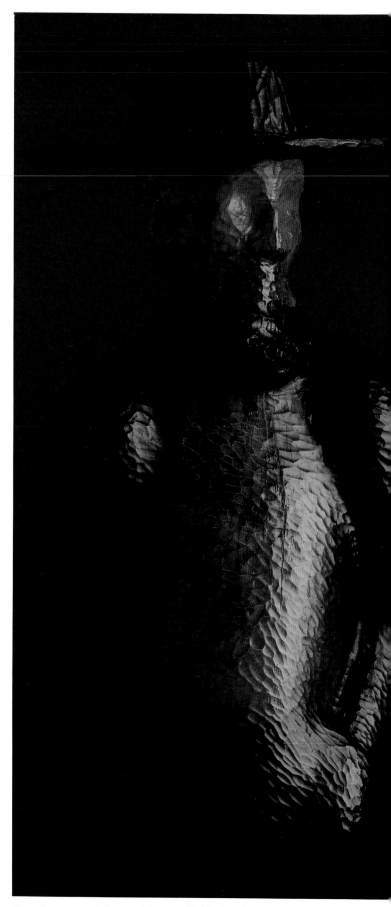

Hostetler and son, Jay, 1959.

The American Man 1962.   *Girl in Red Dress* 1962.

American Son - Jaybird 1962.

The Bather 1958.

Photograph by Monty Calvert

Hostetler with *Girl in Red Dress* 1962.

Date	Name	Material	Finish	Height
1947	Dancers	plaster	smooth, white	
1948	Nude Torso	glazed ceramic	dark & light mottled	12"
1948	Untitled	plaster	painted	
1948	Enju	clay	glazed	1.5'
1948	Untitled	copper wire & wood	smooth	small
1948	Seated female nude	clay modeling		
1948	Untitled	mahogany & wire	smooth	8"
1948	Figure	fired clay		
1948	Head	glazed clay	dark, satiny, smooth	
1948 c.	Head	ceramic	glazed	
1953	Female Torso	clay	glazed	16"
1953	Self-portrait	cast stone		23"
1954	Gestation	plaster	painted	34"
1954 c.	Femme	white plaster	rough	40"
1954	Youth	plaster	smooth, white	4'
1954	Joy	plaster & metal	rough, white	18"
1954	Pater Familias	plaster	rough, some color	18"
1954	He Bold as a Hawk - She Soft as the Dawn	plaster	smooth, white rough	2'
1954	The Meek Jim	plaster	smooth, white	29"
1954	Men Cannot Judge	plaster	white, rough	4'
1955 c.	Patriarch	ceramic		
1955 c.	Small Nude	ceramic		
1955	Stilt Man I	aluminum	rough	1.5'
1955	Portrait of Old Man	plaster	white, surface	18"
1955 c.	Stilt Man II	aluminum	rough	
1955	Archetype	plaster	bronze patina/red	48"
1955	The Skin	aluminum	rough	2'
1955	Patriarch	plaster & alum	rough	2.5'
1955	Head	fired red clay	rough	
1955	Humble Goddess	plaster		32"
1956	Embryo	Georgia pink marble	polished/rough	13"
1956	Newborn	Bedford limestone	polished/rough	18"
1956	The Warrior	Indiana limestone	smooth/rough	2'
1956	Tom Stubbs	terra cotta	rough	18"
1956	Bev	plaster	painted	30"
1956	Crucifix	plaster & oak	smooth	6'
1957	Bouquet Femme	Hocking black walnut	rough	25"
1957	Seated Torso	McGuffy Elm	smooth	25"
1957	Mahogany Torso	African Mahogany	smooth	26"
1957	Torso	sassafras	rough	18"
1957	Sycamore Torso	Hocking sycamore	smooth	27"
1957	Sycamore Torso	Hocking sycamore	smooth	26"
1957	Sleeping Bird	white marble	polished/rough	20"

Date	Name	Material	Finish	Height
1957 c.	Sleeping Bird	ceramics	rough	
1957	Dying Bird	B&W New York Marble		20"
1957	Woman Forms	Hocking sycamore	smooth	26"
1957	Woman	Coolville sassafras	gouge marks	18"
1957 c.	Pátriarch	sculpt metal	rough	
1957 c.	Stilt Man	sculpt metal	rough	
1957	Kopf (or Kopt)	cast stone	smooth	
1957	Persona	solid bronze	polished	38"
1957 c.	Standing Figure	plaster	rough	
1957	Standing Figure	bronze	rough	14"
1957	Standing Woman I	Mexican mahogany	rough	35"
1957	Standing Woman I	bronze		10"
1957	Standing Woman II			9"
1957	Dancing Woman	plaster	some texture	46"
1957	Fallen Figure (Woman)	plaster		16" (32" long)
1957	Siren	mahogany	smooth	28"
1958 c.	Torso			
1958	Torso	solid bronze	rough patina	9"
1958	A Young Woman	mahogany		26"
1958	A Young Woman	mahogany		22"
1958	Standing Figure	plaster	epoxy coating	42"
1958	Standing Figure I	solid bronze	polished	14"
1958	Standing Figure II	bronze	gold patina	10"
1958	Standing Woman	solid bronze	clay modeled	10"
1958	Standing Woman	coco-bolo		25"
1958	Standing Figure I	bronze	polished	14"
1958	Standing Woman III (Walking Woman)	bronze	green patina	8"
1958	Standing Figure (Standing Woman)	Georgia pink marble	rough/smooth	22"
1958	Woman Walking	Mexican mahogany	texture	37"
1958	Seated Woman	plaster	white, rough	23"
1958	Seated Woman	bronze	modeled	9"
1958	Woman Seated	bronze	modeled	13"
1958	Contorted Woman	bronze	modeled	16"
1958	Womanform	elm		24"
1958	Woman Forms)	poplar	polychrome	32"
1958 c.	Woman	McGuffy Elm		25"
1958 c.	Floating Figure	bronze	modedled	
1958	Floating Figure I	bronze	textured	
1958	Floating Figure II	bronze	textured	
1958	Floating Figure III	aluminum	textured	
1958	Woman Rising	bronze	modeled	16"
1958	Floating Woman	aluminum		13"

CHRONOLOGY ONE

Date	Name	Material	Finish	Height
1958	Reclining Forms of a Woman	bronze		14"
1958	Fallen Figure (Fallen Woman?)	bronze		13"
1958	Fallen Woman	solid cast aluminum		8"
1958	Woman Resting	McGuffy Elm	little gouge marked	30"
1958	Reclining Woman	Burnt Elm	smooth, no gouges	36"
1958	Woman Resting	bronze	rough surface	9"
1958	Reclining Figure	black walnut	gouge marks	40"
1958	Reclining Nude	bronze	blue-green patina	12"
1958	Woman Resting	bronze	mottled, like clay	12"
1958	Fallen Man (Death of a Poet, Dying Poet)	McGuffy Elm	smooth	42"
1958	Death of a Poet	bronze	modeled	11"
1958	Martyr (Protest)	alabaster	smooth	18"
1958	A Protest	bronze	archetype textured	18"
1958	A Male Archtype	bronze	textured	9"
1958	A Quiet Man	McGuffy Elm	white gesso	20"
1958	W. H. McGuffy	McGuffy Elm	gouge mark texture	17"
1958	Chimera	ash	polychrome	40"
1958	Fighting Cock	bronze	modeled clay	9"
1959	Protest	black walnut	rough	6.5'
1959	Nature Forms	coco-bolo	smooth	36"
1959	Nature Form	black walnut	smooth	40"
1959	Gibson Girl	black walnut	rough	28"
1959	Entwined Figures	mahogany	smooth	35"
1959	A Young Mother	coco-bolo	smooth	30"
1959 c.	Sleeping Bird	B&W marble	smooth	17"
1959	Seated Woman	black walnut	smooth	48"
1959	Seated Women	elm	smooth	24"
1959	Seated Woman	burnt elm	amooth	24"
1959	Standing Figure	elm	smooth	
1959	Young Queen	ebony	smooth	14"
1959 c.	Fallen Woman	bronze		
1960 c.	Standing Figure	bronze		
1960	Standing Woman	black walnut		6.5'
1960 c.	Warrior	limestone	smooth	
1960 c.	Warrior	scrap metal		
1960	Martyr	elm	gouge marked	2.5'
1960	Morass	woodcut		
1960	Bather	bathbarra	smooth	2.5'
1960	The Bather	coco-bolo	smooth	30"
1960	Figure Forms	mahogany	gouge texture	27"
1960	Figure Forms	poplar	rough	20"
1960	Young Woman	mahogany	some gouge marks	26"
1960	Americana ll	elm	gouge marks	5'
1960	Heritage	black walnut	gouge marks	6.5'

Date		Name	Material	Finish	Height
1960		Heritage	black walnut & marble	gouge marks	47"
1960		Heritage Forms	elm	gouge marks	78"
1961		Griffin	plaster	textured	6'
1961		American Bather			
1961		Standing Woman	elm		46"
1962 c.		Menorah	walnut		24"
1961 c.		Americana I	elm		36"
1962 c.		Martyr	black walnut	gouge marks	70"
1950		Cubist Style Head	bronze	deep brown patina	22"
1985		Cubist Style Head	bronze	patina	22"
1985		Cubist Woman	bronze	deep brown patina	19"
1985		Cubist Woman	bronze	deep brown patina	19"
1985		Bronze Pottery Form	bronze	brown patina	6"
1985		Bronze Pottery Form	bronze	brown patina	6"
1985		Bronze Pottery Form	bronze	brown patina	10"
1985		Bronze Pottery Form	bronze	prown patina	
1972		Maid of Nantucket	black walnut	oxide color dress	38"
1972		Maid of Nantucket	chestnut	natural wood finish	38"
1961	1	Gotham Girl	elm	painted	34"
1962	2	American Lady	elm	polychrome	34"
1962	3	American Man (Amish)	maple	polychrome	40"
1962	4	Girl in a Red Dress	elm	polychrome	42"
1962	5	American Woman (American Beauty)	elm	analine dye	42"
1962	6	American Son	elm	polychrome	39"

Hostetler in Barstow House Studio, 1963.

Off To New York City

Chapter III

American Beauty 1963.

Jim Dine, born in Cincinnati in 1935, was one of David Hostetler's students, but in many respects the roles were reversed. Dine, who is now in the American art history books as a "Pop"artist who was also involved in Happenings and Environments, first visited David at his studio on Highland Avenue David remembers their meeting this way:

"Jim came up one night when I had the windows painted black and the blue lights on. The sculpture is there, the drums are there — I was into African tribal drums then — and I played a record of Moses Asch, Folkways records. I just played drum music on my stereo, much like I do today. So Jim arrived and we beat the drums, sang and danced. When I moved to the farm and had the studio, we would have anti-tension nights — AT Nights, we called them. We'd turn on the blue lights, there would be music and people writhing on the floor. It might have had something to do with those Happenings that Jim picked up with Allan Kapro."

Dine visited the farm almost daily and used a chicken coop as a makeshift studio. Ambitious and energetic, an avid student of the New York art scene, he scoured Art Digest magazine at the OU library for news of contemporary art. He wanted to go to New York. Soon David was loading up his 1949 green Plymouth station wagon with Dine and other students on Friday afternoons for eleven-hour drives to New York City to visit art museums and catch exhibition openings. "Dine had the chutzpah and I had the wheels."

David explained, "We'd get there about 2 A.M. Saturday and locate an ex-OU student to stay with. Then we would do the art scene. During that time I met Red Grooms and Claes Oldenburg and all those people down in the Village. Jim introduced me to Raoul Hague, whose wood sculptures I liked. Jim just smelled them out." When David and June's son was born in 1957, he was named Jay Douglas, or JD as in Jim Dine.

In 1989, Dine, known as a bit of a recluse, rejected a request for an interview, but did mail a note from France to this writer saying, "Hostetler, when I knew him, was a great guy and we listened to some

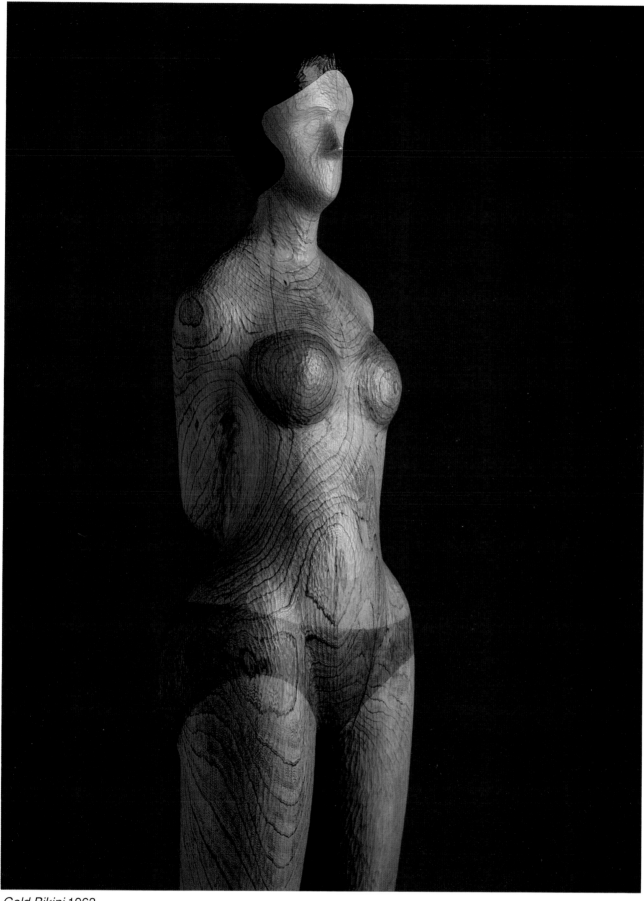

Gold Bikini 1963.

Karsh portrait of Hostetler in Coolville Ridege Studio #1 with *American Daughter - Anne*, 1966.

Photography by
Karsh of Ottawa

Yousuf Karsh, a leading interpretive portrait photographer involved with Ohio University as an adjunct professor in photography, was among the many noted photographers that were excited by the visual talent of Hostetler and his sculptures. This 1960s friendship with Karsh and the other photographers that focused on Hostetler's work, is a key resource for the record of his artistic talent.

Hostetler, Karsh and *Mrs. Alden* in Coolville, 1966.

Hostetler and Karsh at Harmon Gallery Opening, 1967.

American Daughter - Anne, 1965.

Hostetler with *Orange Dress*, 1965.

*American Lady.*1962.

Orange Dress 1965, *American Queen* 1966, *Red Dress* 1965, *Gold Dress* 1965.

Photographs by Fred Schnell

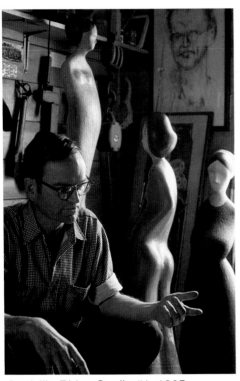

Coolville Ridge Studio #1, 1965.

Hostetler and Sculpture on Coolville Ridge, 1965.

1965, Carving *Walking Woman*

Photograph by David Gilmore

photographs (4) by Dana Vibberts

"Walking Woman"

Studio #2 on Coolville Ridge, 1966.

1965 with "American Woman"

American Woman 1965

Hostetler and Women, 1966.

Hostetler and Women, 1966

American Queen 1966, *Standing Woman* 1965.

American Queen 1966.

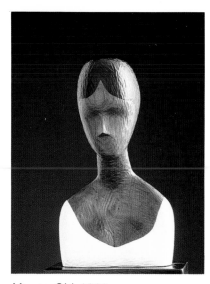

Young Girl 1968

White Stocking 1965.

American Woman 1966

Photograph by Jon Webb

American Woman, Red Stockings, and Seated Woman 1965.

American Beauty 1967.

wonderful music together." The envelope did not have a return address.

But the chicken coop arrangement didn't work out. David recalled, "Jim was not a gracious person and June really disliked him being there. He sort of took over. He did a portrait of our daughters, Janie and Annie, and also one of me that is demented looking. It probably looks quite a bit like me. I remember June saying 'You'll probably grow into that.'

David's mode of dress during the 1950s — he most often didn't wear a tie — was one of the problems that was threatening his chances of getting tenure at the university. His playing drums in a jazz combo and his fraternization with students also didn't help.

University President John Calhoun Baker was of the old school. Professors were to be dignified and wear suits and ties. David recalled, "John Baker scared the hell out of me. He was just like my father - a very stern disciplinarian. Going to see Baker was like going to see my Dad. It was traumatic."

Filled with nervous anticipation of their meeting in Cutler Hall, David would pause outside in the adjacent garden to gather up his courage. The garden, which David called his Gethsemane, is now the site of a Hostetler sculpture.

"Baker would say to me, 'Now, David, about this jazz. You are playing jazz and fraternizing with students. In fact, you give a new dimension to the word fraternization!'"

David had managed to be excused from not wearing ties by simply explaining that if he wore one while bending over a potter's wheel, the tie could get caught in the clay and he could choke to death.

He also couldn't deny the fraternization charge. He had played drums in a jazz combo at fraternity parties and had enjoyed drinks with the party-goers. And there was also that time when he drove a dump truck filled with students out into the country to dig for clay. When rain began pouring, the crew stopped at Pat's Bar in Nelsonville for beers. When they returned to Athens their arrival was no secret on Court Street. The truck rumbled through town with David at the wheel and the pie-eyed students in back singing their lungs out.

In the spring of 1957, after sweating through another tense session with President Baker, David finally received tenure. It had taken him seven years — the maximum time allowable. In the art department tenure was based on competence. David was deemed competent, although in retrospect he now thinks Baker may have just been sympathizing with June.

"We had two little girls; June was head of the blood bank and active in the Episcopal Church," said David. "I don't know for sure but I can bet a millon to one that if I had been single, I wouldn't have been at OU even five years.

In 1957 David also completed his first wood carving, entitled Torso, which had a Hague-like massiveness about it. It was a female torso, the first of what would become almost an exclusively female sculptural obsession.

In 1958 David entered a contest and was delighted to learn that he had won it. The prize: a free exhibition of his sculpture at a New York gallery. The 49 Plymouth was again loaded up with carvings, and off he went with student Dennis Dorogi to The City. As they approached the gallery's address they noticed that the neighborhood looked seedy. They found the second floor gallery, began unloading the sculptures and then got a look at the exhibition contract. Yes, he had won the show, but the opening, food and advertising would cost him $500. He remembered, "I was making $4,000 a year as a teacher. I couldn't afford the show. I yelled to Denny to stop unloading, and told the guy at the gallery I was leaving. I was disconsolate. It was raining, we were wet. We piled everything back in the car and began driving up Madison Avenue to a place we were crashing for the night when we noticed across the street the Avant Garde Gallery. We went in. I told the woman behind the desk my litany of depression and anger and how I was being screwed by the system, when she said, `Wait a minute, Mr. Davis has to hear this.' The gallery owner, Bernard Davis was called downstairs to hear my story. I started in again, and he was so involved in enjoying it he said, `Let's see the work.' So Denny went out and started bringing it in while I continued raving about the system and suddenly Davis says, `I'll give you a show. I like what you've got here.' He gave me a free show. I couldn't believe it."

At the time David was carving abstract sculptures. Some would start out figurative and end up unrecognizable. One, entitled *Chimera*, resembled a standing bird-like creature with a long neck and pyramidal head. It was painted blue and red. The colors reminded Davis of Pennsylvania Dutch folk art.

David took to heart what Davis said, and although he continued to create abstract works, the idea of folk art started sinking into his thoughts. He became tired of the direction he was taking, so in the summer of 1960 stopped carving for almost a year and a half.

He began reading Thoreau on nature, Louis Bromfield on organic farming, books on folk arts, and started collecting antique tools, butter molds, figureheads, anything from the rural American folk heritage. The Hostetlers began raising cattle and chickens, and using horses to plow.

In an interview with the *Kenyon Review* in 1969, David looked back to those back-to-nature years. He said, "It may appear to be a retrogression of some sort to look back to find out where you were in order to find out where you now are. I guess that's what it amounted to. I farmed with the most primitive tools, not because others weren't available but because the quest was to find myself in purest terms."

By 1961 he carved *Gotham Girl*, later named *Nantucket Woman*. It resembled an antique cast iron bootjack called Naughty Nellie that he had hanging on his studio wall, although at the time he hadn't noticed the connection. While Nellie had her legs spread (to allow a boot wearer to grip the heel) *Gotham Girl* was standing primly with her legs together and her hands tucked under her ample bosom. She was wearing dark stockings to above her knees and her bathing suit looked somewhat turn-of-century except for the strapless top.

David was so delighted with the result that he remembers literally jumping up and down with joy.

"I realized that by painting on sculpture - for example, the bathing suit on the surface, you are creating the illusion of different forms on top of forms. Perhaps it was obvious, but for me it was a breakthrough."

Although *Gotham Girl* was overweight and folksy, she was really the beginning of the American Woman, the series of sculptures on which Hostetler's fame mainly rests. And it was the beginning of a distinctive, folklike American style of sculpture that was undeniably Hostetler.

A Champion Appears

In January 1962, a thirty-eight-year-old educator from Harvard came to the Athens campus to take over as university president. A dynamic non-conformist himself, Vernon R. Alden befriended David Hostetler and enjoyed the idea of the sculptor not wearing a necktie to a reception.

During Alden's seven-year tenure, Ohio University was put on the map. Between 1962 and the fall quarter of 1968, enrollment at the university doubled from 10,800 to 22,500; faculty appointments rose from 341 to 736. New red brick dormitories resembling Harvard buildings added to a "Harvard on the Hocking" image. Ohio University had its own "air force" of nine planes donated as tax write-offs by major industries, and nine pilots.

A Chicago native, Alden was a go-getting wonder boy of higher education. A Phi Beta Kappa at Brown, holder of a MBA from Harvard, he was awarded seven honorary doctor's degrees from other universities. At OU, he was appointed by President Lyndon Johnson to be chairman of the Task Force committee planning the U.S. Job Corps. Alden and OU did not go unnoticed. Feature articles about both were carried in *Life*, *Time*, *Newsweek* and the *Wall Street Journal*.

In Hostetler's mind, Alden was also a savvy pro in the fields of public relations and marketing.

"Alden instituted a star system at OU," recalled Hostetler. "I was lucky to be one of the artists he helped . He was a stimulant. He liked my sculpture enough to own it and he flew me around the country to art show openings. He totally supported artistic effort. To him, the arts were high profile. He liked to say that owning a Hostetler was a status symbol and he took pride in helping to promote my work."

During Alden's administration, special guests of the university were frequently taken out to Coolville Ridge to tour Hostetler's studio. When university trustees met, their spouses would go on the tour.

So Alden, the star of higher education, was making Hostetler a star of the art world. Art galleries owned by OU alums were giving Hostetler exhibitions with special openings for other alums.

Alden left Ohio University to become chairman of the board of The Boston Company, a post he held for ten years. He is now on the boards of ten large corporations.

"My wife, Marion, and I look back on those Ohio University years as our happiest days because you had a sense then that you could accomplish almost anything.

W hen I first saw David's work in 1962 I was very much attracted to it because it was a very wholesome kind of art. Because of my longtime interest in Japan, I was very much attracted to the cleanness of his sculpture. Shortly after we arrived, I was surprised to find that David had made a figure that had a hair style patterned after my wife's. He called it Marion Alden and we bought it and still have it. It is a full-length figure and is lean and small and, of course, people could tell it represented my wife. When people came to our home and saw it, they'd become excited about David's work and, I think, he was able to sell quite a bit of his work as a result of that.

"David met Arthur Harris, who was the head of the Meade Corporation Packaging Group, at our home. I was on the board of directors of Meade. Arthur had a process of coloring paper and wood and he and David had an animated conversation about it. Afterwards, David started applying color on his wooden pieces using Arthur's color dye.

"I felt David was one of the stars in our college of fine arts and that we ought to do everything we could to enhance his reputation.

"I had a number of friends from my Harvard Business School days who volunteered to help on different projects. One fellow, Dan Edelman, was fascinated by David and, as a result, Dan's public relations firm helped David free of charge.

"Of course, David is also a tremendous promoter. And a fascinating and very likable personality."

The downside of boosting the sculptor from Beach City to celebrity status was the simmering resentment felt by his older colleagues in the art department.

Hostetler recalled, "Since I was producing, I got the rewards. The people who weren't producing were some of the senior members in the department. I was hated by some of them because they were bypassed. In fact, during the sixties - I forget which year - the university did not give a distinguished professor award because I was put up for it. The heat was so heavy that it was the only year in OU's history that an award wasn't given."

However, there were plenty of others in Athens who regarded Hostetler with awe and admiration.

For example, David Baker, who since 1987 has been the director of the Ohio Department of Development in Columbus, was a business major at OU in the sixties and remembers Hostetler well.

Baker reflected, "I was being taught that in business, you have a career and you can find yourself in that career; that some day later you will do some kind of community work — serve on a symphony board or something — and THAT'S all there is to life.

But as a nineteen-year-old kid at OU, I was meeting this guy Hostetler who created very accomplished artwork which sold and had value, who also taught — and that was having two jobs simultaneously — and he also played drums in a band and rode a motorcycle. He was doing all kinds of things that I was taught that people typically can't do. He was able to integrate what seemed like dozens of different things into a fabric of life that certainly had its problems but also had its fun.

"Hostetler was a hippie before there were such people as hippies. He was his own avant-garde person; and his style — the art, music, the do-your-own-thing philosophy — eventually became sort of de rigueur. And he finally fit. The world caught up with him."

It may be assuming too much to say that Hostetler's life style influenced Baker's. However the fabric of Baker's life includes the following: serving in the Peace Corps in the Philippines, marriage, teaching junior and senior high school, watching a business he helped to start grow from forty employees to ten thousand in seventeen years, retiring to study anthropology at Ohio State, and taking the cabinet post in Governor Richard Celeste's administration. He is the only cabinet member who rides to work on a motorcycle.

Amish or Not?

Much confusion and misinformation has been associated with the Amish influence on the work of David Hostetler. He is the first to admit that Bernard Davis suggested the connection and he simply became interested in the Amish, who were related to him three generations previously. He did appreciate their simple life and was trying out, to some degree, their life style on the farm.

In the *Kenyon Review* article he was asked about whether he was Amish, and he responded, "No, not at all. But I definitely do have the feeling that there is a spiritual quality to everything. There is some spiritualness, intrinsic quality, to every object. And the fact that the tree is a living thing — relates to me as a living thing — in that sense, it's definitely spiritual, whether you call it religious or not."

The Amish connection was jumped on as more Hostetler exhibitions were mounted. It was a "hook" that art writers and critics could grab and go with. It was a fresh angle — something new to write about. David, learning more and more about the necessity of proper publicity — something he saw Jim Dine doing successfully — did not discourage the Amish angle.

Another name was applied to David's work — Pop Provincial. It blended right in with the Warhol-Dine-Oldenburg Pop Art scene of the 1960s, but the name, however descriptive, never stuck.

Time magazine's review of a May, 1965, Sculpture Center Gallery exhibition in New York included these words: "... the sculptor's Amish folk, bathing beauties and long-gowned ladies all look as if they had come from the sticks for a day in the big town. And so they have. They are fresh from Hostetler's Ohio farm, where he chopped down his own elm trees, chipped them out, dolled them up with paint, and packed them off for their first visit to New York. They'll never go back."

Yet there was another side to this Amish interest, one that two of David's friends questioned. The late Tony Trisolini, Dean of the College of Fine Arts for whom the OU gallery is now named, saw David's black-dressed Amish figures in a show and, according to David, "came out yelling, 'Shades of Cotton Mather!'

"I didn't even know who Cotton Mather was. I had to look it up. I began to realize that I had unknowingly brought forth in my sculpture these black-clad, Calvinist-screaming figures. I was even painting the handles of my carving tools black, like the way the Amish paint their buggy bumpers. Everything chrome or colorful I painted black."

A New York painter named Dick Steinberg, whom David had met while teaching one summer in Mexico, came into his Athens studio and commented, "Jesus Christ, everything's black! You've got names like 'Martyr' and 'Crucifix' and you've got this beautiful place you're living on! You've got a great life! What the hell are you martyred about?"

David began to wonder what he was "climbing on the cross about."

"It would take a shrink to delve into that," he admits. "My father had told me the Amish were not noble. They were pacifists for one thing, and my father was a great flag waver. So the Amish were never held up to me as positive. When I returned to the Amish thing it was with mixed emotions. I remembered my Grandpa George and the chicken on his lap — the idea of self-sufficiency, the return to the earth thing. There was a commune north of Athens that was a co-counseling group. One listens and the other talks and vice versa. And usually it's the traumas that you suffered in childhood that are not resolved. They keep coming back and keep coming back because you haven't gone through them. These fears, these things, the martyrs, black-dressed figures, perhaps that's what this art was for me — a way to get it out. I can get my projections, my fantasies out in a healthy way through the art."

David noted that in his youth it was always the women, such as Grandma Penrod, who were tender and kind. "In my sculptures the male figures — martyrs, the dying poet — represent something not too pleasant. But the women represent something very pleasant, very sensual, soft, nurturing, fulfilling while the male is hard, dying, hurt, wounded."

With that deeply ingrained outlook on the sexes, is it any wonder that the American Woman has become Hostetler's sole sculptural subject since the late 1960s?

The Hostetler Hype and Hippies are Born

Hostetler's sculptures were featured in thirty-seven art exhibitions during the 1960s in such places as New York, Chicago, Miami, Cincinnati, Columbus, Cleveland, Dayton, Detroit, Fort Lauderdale, Sarasota, Boston, San Francisco, Macon, and Oshkosh.

By now he was good copy to newspaper and magazine writers. They described not only his artwork, but his use of hip jargon, his drum-playing in a jazz combo, the university paying him well as a full professor and his jetting to gallery openings around the country.

He was invited to appear on the television quiz show "To Tell The Truth." He wryly remembers the experience this way: "They gave me free airplane tickets to and from New York. It was first class to New York and coach back home. That sums up the experience."

Fred Schnell wrote in the *Columbus Dispatch* Sunday Magazine in 1966, "The free-thinking youngsters at the university gather around him, admiring his unaffectedness and realizing that the same simple compassion in his art enables him to understand their problems. Their admiration for his talent and feeling is intensified by the belief that Hostetler is an individual; and through his individuality in some way has beaten "the system."

The system that he seemed to be beating was, in one sense, the system the young people in the next few years would be protesting about in demonstrations and love-ins. Youths would protest against the military/industrial complex escalating the Vietnam War, the big money bosses in their white collar jobs and their conservative values."

Haight-Ashbury in San Francisco was a big topic in the news. Hippies there smoked pot. Young people fled the midwest to go there. In Cleveland a coffee house in a church was shut down by police because a poet there used sexual obscenities in his poems. Hair became a hit. Communes and Woodstock were around the corner.

In the art world too there was protest. Angry artists were making earth sculptures that no one could buy and tuck neatly in their living room. The New York art scene was viewed as a place where artist, critics, dealers and museum curators were in a conspiracy, deciding what art to push that year. Certain art, like fashion, was "in" one year and "out" the next.

Hostetler told the *Kenyon Review* in 1969: "The only thing that bothers me is the fact that New York is so singular, so one-track. Whatever they're on at the moment is the total style. And everything becomes total then, all the journalism, the fashion, everything becomes directed to that particular style, so much so that it excludes everything else. And this to me is a very unhealthy condition. How can something be everything today when tomorrow you know it will be nothing in their eyes? It has to be somewhat postulated on an economic throne. Otherwise why would you handle things that way? New York ought to take a more Oriental approach and recognize that everything has some value."

Today, David, in reconsidering what he said nearly twenty years ago, laughs about it and admits, "There may have been some sour grapes in what I said. But New York, the hype, the instant fame and the rat race only confused me. I read what people wrote about me and tried to be what they said I was. Finally, I couldn't take it. I was frightened. I made the only move I could see to make, and that was to retreat. So I came back to Athens and my farm to regroup. Here I know who I am. I can feel total. I can be me."

Churchill, Hemingway and Now David Hostetler

By the mid-1960s David Hostetler's ever-growing number of carved figures were not only being sought by collectors but were being viewed as subjects or props for advertising.

A glimpse of a seated Hostetler figure can be seen in the 1966 film, *The Group*, a drama based on the Mary McCarthy novel about the ongoing relationships of Vassar graduates.

A camera crew from Detroit descended on the Hostetler farm in 1967 to photograph the carved ladies lounging around the newest American motors automobile. David recalls that the motor of the brand-new car had burned out on its way to the farm and a tow truck was required to move the car about the field for the proper poses.

Also that year one of the world's most famous photographers, a man who had created classic portraits of Churchill, Hemingway and Eisenhower, was invited to Ohio University and met Hostetler. They instantly hit it off. Their friendship resulted in a unique joint exhibition of sculpture and photographs, certainly one of David's most memorable shows. It received high praise in Boston, New York and Naples and Sarasota, Florida.

Yousuf Karsh and his wife Estrellita are still good friends with David, and get together with him in the summers at David's home in Nantucket.

Karsh wrote a short piece about his 1967 meeting with David in the Ohio Alumnus Magazine. He wrote: "Many links of friendship have brought me into the stimulating family of Ohio University. Soon after Vernon Alden was appointed president of Ohio University, I was invited to Athens as a member of the Fine Arts Visiting Committee.

"One of the people I met on the occasion of my first Athens visit was a gifted teacher and a fine human being, the sculptor David Hostetler. At once, I was drawn to his calm and sincere manner and his quiet dedication to his work. He took me out to his farm and studio, and I was introduced to his sculpture, his 'women.'

"Right then and there, I decided I wanted to photograph him in his own environment with his 'women,' for his original approach to his work, the result of many years of slowly defining his own artistic idiom, impressed me. That he literally worked from the earth, that his 'women' were created from the elm trees which grew on his farm, delighted me. His reverence for, and glory in, woman, his diversified interpretations of her, were compelling. Immediately, we see the goddess, the seductress, the vulnerable creature, the helpmate — indeed, everything that is woman.

"I decided to photograph the artist and his women in their natural setting, and we progressed, in easy stages, from the barn to the studio, to the pasture, to the edge of the pond on his property. So I went with David's women as far as I could — as far as they would let me — to the very brink of the water.

"It was a cold and windy March weekend, but as we worked together, each piece of sculpture became more distinct to me as a separate personality, and soon, they were huddling together speaking intimately to David, bracing themselves against the wind, or joining him in a relaxed gambol near a favorite tree or in striking stances near the coal pile. I was oblivious to the cold and the wind.

"June Hostetler, David's wife, discovered that not only was she playing hostess to my wife and me but also to the suddenly appearing young volunteer photographic assistants who materialized on Coolville Ridge, armed with windbreakers and cameras.

"It was a memorable few days and helped strengthen our fast-growing friendship."

To the Woods, to the Woods

Hostetler's back-to-nature emphasis, his fascination with a simple lifestyle, his follow-your-bliss idea and his revelry in the joys of the creative life resulted in something akin to an artist's colony in the hills east of Athens.

Within ten square miles half a dozen artists and craftsmen began settling in rustic settings. The eldest was John Rood, a wood sculptor whose cosmopolitan life had taken him all over the world since the 1930s, and who wanted to settle again near his home town of Athens. Hostetler helped him buy some hilly land nearby. Rood authored a book on wood sculpture that remained in print for decades.

Jim Garner, who had dropped out of OU in 1960 to join the Army, wrote Hostetler, his former teacher, from Korea asking him to buy for him some land in the hills. Hostetler lined up forty acres in a hollow for one thousand dollars.

The result was that Garner and his artist wife, Sylvia, built a log cabin, where they remained longer than Thoreau did at Walden Pond. Garner carved picture frames and small sculptures and Sylvia painted abstract paintings.

Vern Allen, a former Peace Corps volunteer, settled nearby also and began carving sculptures and furniture. David Baird bought eighty-five acres, fixed up a century-old farm house, installed a kiln and began producing small sculptures for gift shops.

Ron Chacey began using a dozen different kinds of wood to design and make banjo necks and dulcimers. And Kix Stewart returned to the area to duplicate old musical instruments.

Some of Hostetler's former students began building elaborate tree houses and living in them.

Of course, some of these woods dwellers didn't stay the two years and two months that Thoreau stayed at Walden Pond. Yet today, in the hills around Athens small pockets of dedicated do-your-own-thingers can be found. Some call Athens County one of the last bastions of hippiedom. ●

CHRONOLOGY TWO

Date	Piece	Name	Material	Finish	Height
1963	7	American Daughter (Janie)	pine	polychrome	22"
1963	8	American Daughter (Annie)	pine	polychrome	26"
1963	9	Rain Girl (American Woman)	elm	polychrome	47"
1963	10	American Wife (Mennonite Wife, Am. Woman III, June)	elm	polychrome	22"
1963	11	American Bather	spalted elm	polychrome	47"
1963	12	American Girl (Janie)	elm	polychrome	21"
1963	13	American Beauty	elm	polychrome	
1963	14	American Wife (June)	elm	polychrome	48"
1964	15	Red Cloak (Green Cape)	elm	polychrome	42"
1964	16	Green Dress I	elm	polychrome	36"
1965	17	Green Dress II	elm	polychrome	43"
1964	18	American Wife II (Blue Dress)	elm	polychrome	54"
1964	19	American Girl (Yellow Hat)	sassafras	polychrome	51"
1964	20	Plain Woman (Mennonite Woman, Blue Dress)	elm	polychrome	45"
1964	21	Seated Woman	elm	polychrome	30"
1964	22	Red Stockings	elm	polychrome	43"
1965	23	American Wife	elm	polychrome	71"
1965	24	Black Haired Woman	elm	polychrome	25"
1965	25	American Wife (White Dress)	elm	polychrome	64"
1965	26	Orange Dress I	elm	painted	56"
1965	27	Orange Dress II	elm	polychrome	53"
1965	28	American Daughter (Jane)	elm	polychrome	49"
1965	29	White Stockings	elm	polychrome	48"
1965	30	Gold Dress (American Wife /June)	elm	polychrome	49"
1966	30B	Gold Dress	bronze	gold patina	49"
	30W	Gold Dress	dark wood	natural	
	30B	Gold Dress	bronze	dark patina	42"
	30B	Gold Dress	bronze	green patina	
	30B	Gold Dress (American Wife)	bronze	patina	49"
	30B	Gold Dress	bronze	patina	
	30B	Gold Dress	bronze	polished	49"
1965	31	Red Dress	maple	polychrome	62"
1965	32	American Daughter	elm	polychrome	36"
1965	33	Orange Dress III	elm	polychrome	53"
1965	34	American Dream	elm	polychrome	65"
1965	35	Orange Cape	elm	polychrome	56"
1966	36	Yellow Cape (American Son)	elm	polychrome	36"
1966	37	American Queen (Blue Cape)	elm	polychrome	58"
1983	37B	American Queen	bronze	polished	5'6"
1972	37BT	American Queen (bust)	bronze	black painted	22"
1968	37BT	American Queen (bust)	bronze	dark brown patina	22"

Date	Piece	Name	Material	Finish	Height
1969	37BT	American Queen (bust)	bronze	polished	22"
1966	38	White Boots (Rust Cape)	elm	polychrome	36"
1966	39	Yellow Dress (Mrs. Alden)	elm	polychrome	41"
1972	39W	American Woman (Mrs. Alden)	blk walnut	polychrome	42"
1975	39W	American Woman (Mrs. Alden)	box elder	polychrome	43"
1972	39B	American Woman (Mrs. Alden)	bronze	polished	43"
1976	39B	American Woman (Mrs. Alden)	bronze	polished	38"
1979	39B	American Woman	bronze	polished	42"
1969	39B	American Woman	bronze	dark brown patina	41"
1972	39B	American Woman	bronze	dark black patina	41"
1972	39WT	American Woman Torso	black walnut		20"
1972	39WT	American Woman	blk walnut		22.5"
1972	39WT	American Woman	blk walnut	natural	23"
1973	39WT	American Woman	blk walnut	natural	23"
1974	39WT	American Woman	box elder	aniline gold dress	22"
1975	39WT	American Woman	box elder	blue dress	20"
1981	39BT	American Woman	bronze	polished	11"
1981	39BT	American Woman	bronze	polished	15"
1968	39BT	American Woman	aluminum	GTO green/polished	
1973	39BT	American Woman	bronze	polished	16"
1973	39BT	American Woman	bronze	polished	17"
1974	39BT	American Woman	bronze	polished	17"
1976	39BT	American Woman	bronze	polished	16"
1980	39BT	American Woman	bronze	polished	14"
1972	39BT	American Woman	bronze	polished	17"
1966	40	Seated Woman, Orange Dress	elm	polychrome	37"
1966	41	Big Daddy	elm	polychrome	32"
1966	42	Red Shoes	elm	polychrome	38"
1966	43	American Woman (White Hat)	elm	polychrome	48"
1967	44	Gold Dress (Pony Tail)	elm	polychrome	48"
1967	45	American Wife	elm	polychrome	55"
1967	46	Young Woman (Bust)	elm	polychrome	29"
1967	47	Green Dress	elm	polychrome	38"
1967	48	Red Haired Girl	elm	polychrome	28"
1967	49	Pony Tail (Golden Girl)	elm	polychrome	58"
1967	50	Seated Woman (Yellow Dress)	elm	polychrome	37"
1967	51	Red Dress	elm	polychrome	49"
1967	52	White Dress (Red Pony Tail)	elm	polychrome	44"
1973	52W	Pony Tail	walnut	polychrome	47"
1972 c.	52B	Pony Tail	bronze	brown black patina	45"
1973 c.	52B	Pony Tail	bronze	textured	45"
1967	53	Red Stockings	elm	polychrome	42"
1967	54	Long Haired Woman	elm	polychrome	54"
1973 c.	54WT	Bust of Long Haired Girl	basswood	natural	21.5"

Date	Piece	Name	Material	Finish	Height
1974 c.	54B	Long Haired Girl	bronze	rubbed patina	52"
1976	54B	Long Haired Girl	bronze	polished face & neck	52"
1985	54B	Long Haired Woman	bronze		50"
1973	54BT	Long Haired Girl (bust)	bronze	polished patina	22"
1973 c.	54BT	Long Haired Girl	bronze	rubbed patina	22"
1977	54BT	Long Haired girl	bronze	black rubbed patina	22"
1979 c.	54BT	Long Haired Girl	bronze	polished	23"
1967	55	Dancing Woman (Gold dress, Pony Tail)	elm	polychrome	41"
1967	56	American Daughter (Teeny Bopper)	elm	polychrome	36"
1967	57	American Beauty	elm	polychrome	41"
1968	58	Seated Woman (Yellow Dress)	elm	polychrome	42"
1968	59	Standing Woman (One Leg)	willow	carved	36"
1971	59WT	American Girl (from girl on one leg)	red elm	carved	14"
1972	59WT	American Girl	beech	heavy grain markings	14"
1972	59WT	Black Girl	blk walnut	carved	14"
1972	59WT	Black Girl	blk walnut	carved	14"
1972	59WT	Black Girl	blk walnut	carved	14"
1972	59WT	American Girl	oak	natural wood	14"
1972	59BT	American Girl (from girl on one leg)	bronze	carved	14"
1972	59BT	American girl	bronze	polished	13"
1972	59BT	American Girl	bronze	black polished	15"
1972	59BT	American Girl	bronze	polished	15"
1968	60	White Cape (Cape Woman)	oak	carved	41"
1969	60B	Cape Woman	bronze	lt. brown patina	40"
1968	61	American Beauty	elm	polychrome	49"
1968	62	Long Haired Girl (bust)	elm		20"
1968	63	Gold Dress	elm	polychrome	52"
1968	64	White Dress	elm	polychrome	39"
1968	65	Seated Woman	elm	polychrome	27"
1968	66	Standing Woman (American Wife)	elm	polychrome	6'5"
1978	66B	Standing Woman	bronze	wood chip marks	6'7"
1984	66B	Standing Woman	bronze	green patina	7'
1968	67	Walking Woman	elm	polychrome	45"
1968	68	Girl w/ Red Head Band (bust)	elm	polychrome	12"
1968	69	American Woman	elm	polychrome	53"
1968	70	Mrs. Alden II	elm	polychrome	49"
1973	70WT	Woman (bust)	chestnut	polychrome	20"
1982	70B	Quiet Woman	bronze	polished	42"
1982	70B	Quiet Woman	bronze	carved	42"
1984	70B	Quiet Woman	bronze	polished	50"

Date	Piece	Name	Material	Finish	Height
1973	70WT	Sensual Woman (bust)	box elder	polychrome	20"
1973	70WT	Sensual Woman (bust)	box elder	polychrome	19"
1975	70WT	Bust of American Woman	box elder	polychrome	20"
1973	70BT	Bronze Bust (Woman)	bronze	black polished	18"
1973	70BT	Woman (bust)	bronze	green patina	18"
1969	71	Mrs. Alden II /Red Dress	elm	polychrome	32"
1972	71W	Quiet Woman	blk walnut	natural wood	32"
1972	71W	Quiet WOman	maple wood		34"
1973	71W	Quiet Woman	walnut	natural wood	34"
1978	71W	Quiet Woman	white oak	natural wood	47"
1969	71B	Quiet Woman	bronze	brown patina	34"
1972	71B	Quiet Woman	bronze	polished	35"
1976	71B	Quiet Woman	bronze	polished	33.5"
1977	71B	Quiet Woman	bronze	polished	33.5"
1978	71B	Quiet Woman	bronze	polished	33"
1979	71B	Quiet Woman	bronze	polished	45"
1985	71B	Quiet Woman	bronze	dark brown patina	33"
1981	71B	Quiet Woman	bronze	carved polished	33"
1980	71B	Quiet Woman	bronze	green patina	33"
1972	71BT	Quiet Woman (bust)	chestnut		15"
1973	71WT	Quiet Woman (bust)	box elder		14"
1975	71WT	Quiet Woman (bust)	box elder		21.5"
1975	71WT	Quiet Woman (bust)	blk walnut	natural wood	19"
1978	71WT	Quiet Woman (bust)	beech	polychrome	18"
1979	71WT	Quiet Woman (bust)	beech	polychrome	16"
1979	71WT	Quiet WOman (bust)	box elder	polychrome	19"
1980	71WT	Quiet Woman (bust)	beech	polychrome	18"
1982	71WT	Quiet Woman (bust)	elm	polychrome	13"
1982	71BT	Quiet Woman (bust)	maple	polychrome	18.5"
1982	71WT	Quiet Woman (bust)	maple		17"
1982	71WT	Quiet Woman	maple	smooth sanded	17.5"
		Nantucket Woman			
1983	71WT	Nantucket Woman	cedar	smooth	18"
1973	71BT	Quiet Woman (bust)	bronze	green patina	15"
1973	71BT	Quiet Woman (bust)	bronze	green patina	11"
1973	71BT	Quiet Woman (bust)	bronze	polished	13"
1976	71BT	Quiet Woman (bust)	bronze	dark black patina	13"
1976	71BT	Quiet Woman (bust)	bronze	black patina	14"
1976	71BT	Quiet Woman (bust)	bronze	black patina	14"
1973	71BT	Quiet Woman (bust)	bronze	polished	15"
1973	71BT	Quiet Woman (bust)	bronze	polished	15"
1974	71BT	Quiet Woman (bust)	bronze	polished	14"
1975	71BT	Quiet Woman (bust)	bronze	polished	16"
1981	71BT	Quiet Woman (bust)	bronze	polished	16"
1976	71BT	Quiet Woman (bust)	bronze	polished	16"

Standing Girl 1968.

Art Park, Haven For The Non-Ego?

Chapter IV

In 1970, Hostetler and two other OU art teachers, George Kokis and David Klahn and former student, Vern Allen, formed a non-profit, educational organization called Art Park Inc. to administer an idealistic and experimental project that never quite worked out.

The idea was to establish a park in a wide hollow on the edge of Coolville Ridge, an area junked up with car body debris and strip-mined earth but also featuring one impressive natural formation, a large rock cliff. It would become Art Park, where artists, inspired by the natural setting, could create new art forms. An Art Park Festival would be held there for four days in May. The cliff would serve as a back drop to what could become a natural amphitheater possibly seating five thousand.

Hostetler was careful to point out to concerned Athens citizens that nothing like another Woodstock was planned.

Art Park had no connection with Ohio University. Klahn, also a sculptor and an assistant professor of art, said, however, that the park was a "natural extension of the art school and a public park for a city that never had one."

The forty-acre park was owned by Hostetler and sculptor Vern Allen, who by then was an instructor at the Philadelphia College of Art.

Donations were needed, industries were to be solicited for funds or in kind services, and *Life* magazine, composer John Cage and sculptor Frank Gallo were reportedly interested in the project.

A project description noted that the May festival would serve as a pause in the structuring of the park "to celebrate life and the right to be alive and of the species 'people.'"

The festival was held and attracted a number of artists and teachers from such places as California, Oregon, Michigan and New York who arrived to create unique nature-oriented projects.

The Cleveland Press account, titled "Park is testing ground for artists' new works" said "Red-bearded Graham Metson, an English artist who has exhibited works for fifteen years in New York, recently sold his Silver Cloud Rolls Royce. He no longer paints. He looked at a raw scar of bulldozed earth in Art Park and said, "I want to spray a mixture of mulch, manure and seed on that hill to make it green. That

Art Park, 1971, Faye and David Klahn.

David Hostetler with *Standing Girl*, 1968.

has the elements of earth returning to earth. I don't want to leave anything behind to identify me. The world should be nicer where we have worked. Scarred earth is my bag."

The entrance to the park was a tubular archway with "Art Park" spelled out on top in flickering light bulbs, the creation of OU sculpture student Tom Taylor. Another student, Richard Robideau, dangled a pole from the top of a tree. At the end of the pole was a pencil that would draw patterns on large sheets of paper as the wind blew the tree top. Another student created a yarn house around a circle of saplings. Raku kilns were built to make pottery, and John Spofforth used bricks to make twisted walls. Large balloons were inflated to appear like massive snakes burrowing into the ground. Car bodies were welded together into a huge totem pole. Free-form jazz was played in the amphitheater. Those at the festival seemed to be having a good time.

However, the local Board of Health did not approve of the water system and the number of toilet facilities. Sewers would have to be put in. The potential wasn't met. Discouragement abounded. Disillusionment reigned. The project died. A year after it opened, *The Athens Messenger* quoted Hostetler as saying he had had his fill of hassles from the Health Department, which had forbidden large gatherings of people at Art Park because of insufficient sewage and water systems.

"There are ways to get around the Health Department ruling, Hostetler explained, such as decreasing the expected number of visitors, and thereby reducing the required number of outhouses, but the sculptor feels it would be too costly to explore them in terms of legal fees, time and energy," said *The Messenger* story.

Today, Hostetler recalls, "Art Park was supposedly a non-ego place where you found yourself — where you worked as a group for the betterment of the group. It was just wonderfully sophomoric, a great ideal. But it was a lot of fun for me, even though it was probably the most naive thing I did in my life.

"The positive part about it was trying to do an art that had a low ego quotient on it on which people didn't sign their name, where art wasn't so heavily an extension of their personal ego. That was the first step where I went wrong. No artist that I know is egoless. If you are egoless, one thing that you aren't is an artist.

"Four students at Kent State were killed on May 4th and while the Art Park Festival was going on a rock fan was murdered at the Altamont Rock Festival. Athens is a very quiet rural community and so for good reason the citizens of Athens thought I was creating a guerrilla warfare camp for students to take over the city. Of course, it wasn't true. But now what's left of Art Park is grown over and neglected. Robideau's tree was chopped down. I guess even that chopped-down tree is some sort of aesthetic statement.

The idea of environmental art in the wilds of Athens County —an idea spawned by Art Park — has not died out however. In 1981, for example, the Hocking Valley Art Council and Ohio Arts Council supported a Spring Fever Festival in May that featured, besides music, installations that made both political and fanciful statements. Vietnam veteran Don McKinney said something about tension, anxiety and confinement with a work consisting of thousands of sharpened bamboo sticks projecting up from the ground, the kind the Viet Cong used as booby traps. With heavy irony, they were arranged on a small patch of land surrounded by barbed wire and a moat. Artists Mary Manusos and Mel Durand used twigs on a hillside to form the shape of the hull of a ship. Entitled "Land-locked Sailor's Dream," a few wooden pink flamingos

Coolville Ridge Studio #2, 1972.

Quiet Woman 1972.

were stuck about to add a suburban touch while hundreds of blue glass hearts were scattered on the ground. The artists had hoped to leave the hearts there for someone to puzzle over for years to come.

Sculptural Forms: Variations on a Theme

During his intense involvement with Art Park and non-ego art, Hostetler considered giving up the idea of creating art objects, but the thought didn't linger long.

His wooden women began picking up stakes and spending the summers in Nantucket during the 1970s. Hostetler's second wife, Sue Henning, had taught school on the island and had friends there. A summer home was constructed there and Hostetler has exhibited works there every summer since.

One new element to his work was introduced during the energy crunch that began in 1973. Plenty of wood was being burned in fireplaces around Athens and Hostetler started noticing that some of it was spalted. These ultra-thin lines of fungi within the wood created an added decorative element on the surface of his carvings. Hostetler's habit of keeping his gouges sharper than razors enabled him to keep these traceries even with the rest of the surface. Some of his spalted works are among his most attractive pieces.

A summer on the Greek island of Samos in 1975 resulted in another new look to his American Women. He explained, "I realized how long it took the Greeks to get out of the very static sculptural form of the Egyptian totem frontal view and realized it took them centuries to do something that I was actually doing in four decades. So in the middle of the seventies my biggest discovery was to activate my women. After my Greek trip they had more motion and were less static. I think the major thing is that they are reflections of me; art is a mirror image of a person's life discovery. The seventies was a time of finding out about myself.

Walking Woman epitomizes motion. Although it lacks feet and hands, the twist of the body and the flair of the pants legs, as if stopped for a fraction of a second of movement, makes it one of the most endearing and joyful of Hostetler's woman series.

Dancing Woman, a full-gowned figure also conveys forward motion because of the forward position of the pelvis and one leg. Her upward-lifted face and shoulders and her casual arm position, as if her hands were in some invisible pockets, adds an insouciant and charming air to the work. Its C-shaped configuration make it unique among all of Hostetler's works.

Honors and shows have kept coming Hostetler's way up through the eighties. The Nestles Corporation purchased a piece for its headquarters in Toronto. Fanuiel Hall in Boston features a bronze piece, and in April 1989 a sculpture was dedicated at Ohio University — the first outdoor sculpture added to the campus since the Civil War.

Hostetler was given a chapter in the *Masters of Wood Sculpture* book by Nicholas Roukes. Described was the sculptor's controversial technique of carving green wood and keeping it from cracking by "wet wrapping" the piece in plastic and wet rags during storage and between carving sessions. The wrapping also encourages spalting, which Hostetler enjoys having as an added surface feature. He applies five coats of polyurethane which allows water to leave slowly without checking.

Besides the five hundred or more sculptures Hostetler has contributed to the art world, there is also the impact of his teaching to be acknowledged. Two former students remember him vividly.

Photograph by David Perry

Hostetler with *Walking Woman* 1976.

om Taylor, the sculptor of the Art Park gate, and now an art professor of Columbia College in downtown Chicago, noted, "I never remember having had a bad moment with David. As a teacher, he was a patient and caring person who took time with his students. He gave us room to explore. He gave me the opportunity to discover what it was that I wanted to do and helped me define it. He helped me learn how to be a teacher and the importance of having a sense of humor in class. David is celebrating life, literally, and through his art. My art, when it is best for me, is also a celebration of life."

Hugh Burns, who owns a contracting business in Carrollton, Ohio devoted to grooming woodlots for timber production, is a skillful craftsman with a lathe. His wooden bowls and goblets are worked so precisely that light can be seen through their surfaces.

Burns studied fine art at Ohio University and by the summer of 1977 had a teaching assistantship there in woodworking. It was the only summer he spent living in a tree house.

He recalled, "David's son, Jay, and I struck up a friendship, and since I had no money, we shared the tree house in the area called Art Park. It had a loft, a stained glass window, two skylights and a twenty-foot rope ladder up to it in the triple-stem cottonwood tree. I started OU in 1973 when the Vietnam War was winding down. As a teacher, David impressed on me the idea of being true to yourself, to go with what works for you. He kept saying 'Simplify your life, make things as uncomplicated as possible.' So I lived in a tree house that summer.

"What I remember about David was his lust for life, his affinity for nature, for wood, for anything funky and folk. We hit it off. He encouraged me to continue with my lathe work and I'm glad I did. He had an affinity for material and absolute control over it. I strive for that same control. He is inspirational. He made me see things in a light that I had never seen before."

Hostetler in Studio #2 carving *Summertime Woman* 1977.

Burns obviously shares Hostetler's affinity for wood and is helping to ensure a healthy supply of it will be around for decades. Between 1978 and 1988, the Hugh Burns Woodland Improvement Company has planted two million trees.

Burns is among the scores of former Hostetler students who keep in touch by visiting the Coolville Ridge farm to see what new sculptural concept is engaging the master's enthusiasm.

Since retiring in 1985, Hostetler has become extremely prolific. Good health, aided by frequent tennis sessions, has given him a burst of creative energy. The monumental outdoor work now in progress, he hopes, will be the first in a series of new larger-than-life-size pieces.

He hopes to have a foundation at the farm after his death. The limited edition works will continue to be cast until the editions runs out. The farm may well resemble Henry Moore's in England with large sculptures dotting the ffelds.

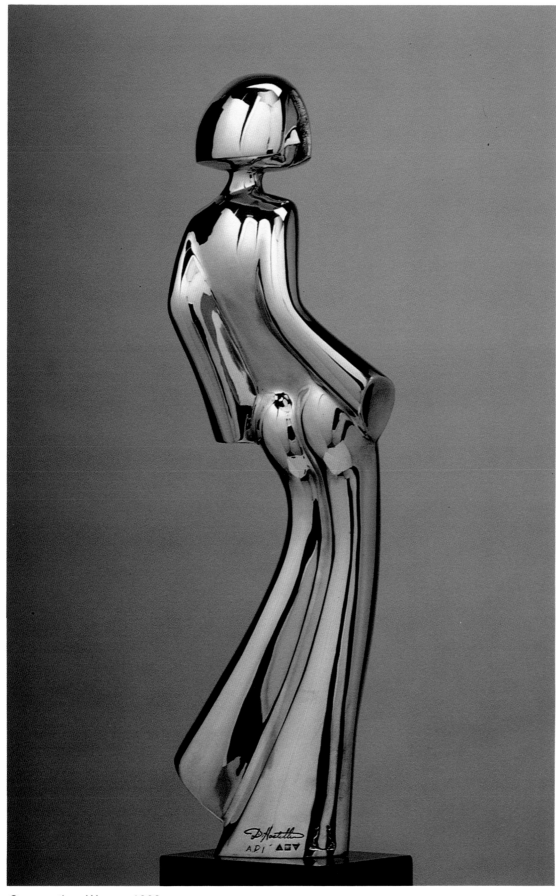

Summertime Woman 1982

He is discovering South American woods with rich colors and bold grains to carve. When completed, the works will show to the world what precious woods are being destroyed in South American rain forests.

He said, "I figure that at my age if you're not doing what you want to do, you're in trouble. My Dad lasted three years after retirement. People get the false idea that when they retire they are going to be free to do what they want to do. When they do retire they realize they don't have anything to do. That must come as a hell of a shock.

"I feel so blessed in not having anything to retire from. This is it! As long as I'm on this planet, I'll be fooling around with clay and plaster and wood and these images that just keep marching out of me.

"I feel blessed. I really do." ●

–Richard Wootten

Photograph by Brian Blauser

Hostetler, 1936 Ford and *American Girl* 1973.

Hostetler in Nantucket Studio carving *Nella* 1974.

David in Athens 1972

Pink Dress 1985, *Dancing Woman* 1979, *Black Woman* 1972,

The Bather 1961, *Summertime Woman* 1982, *Classic Lady* 1983, *American Girl - Lisa* 1983.

Date	Piece	Name	Material	Finish	Height
1976	71BT	Quiet Woman (bust)	bronze	polished	14"
1980	71BT	Quiet Woman (bust)	bronze	polished	15"
1981	71BT	Quiet Woman (bust)	bronze	polished	15"
1982	71BT	Universal Woman (Mrs. Alden)	bronze	polished	17"
1983	71BT	Gold Lady (24K gold plated)	bronze	carved bronze	10"
1981	71BT	Quiet Woman (bust)	nickel silver-plated		12"
1982	71BT	Quiet Woman (unfinished)	bronze	green patina	16.5"
1976	71BT	Quiet Woman (large bust)	bronze	polished	20"
1976	71BT	Quiet Woman (large bust)	bronze	polished	21"
1977	71BT	Quiet Woman (large bust)	bronze	polished	20"
1977	71BT	Quiet Woman (large bust)	bronze	polished	20"
1979	71BT	Quiet Woman (large bust)	bronze	polished	20"
1980	71BT	Quiet Woman (large bust)	bronze	polished	20"
1980	71BT	Serene Woman (large bust)	bronze	polished	18.5"
1981	71BT	Quiet Woman (large bust)	bronze	polished	20"
1981	71BT	Serene Woman (large bust)	silver-plated	bronze	19"
1976	71BT	Quiet Woman (large bust)	bronze	black patina	19"
1969	72	Standing Girl (Flare Skirt)	elm	polychrome	30"29"
1972	72W	Flare Skirt	blk walnut	polychrome	30"
1972	72W	Flare Skirt	elm	polychrome	30"
1972	72W	Flare Skirt	blk walnut	polychrome	30"
1973	72W	Flare Skirt	blk walnut	natural	29"
1978	72W	Flare Skirt	sassafras	natural	27"
1982	72W	Flare Skirt	spltd. black walnut		9"
1973	72B	Flare Skirt	bronze	polished dress	29"
1973	72B	Flare Skirt	bronze	yellow-green patina	30"
1980	72B	Flare Skirt	bronze	polished/textured	29"
1983	72B	Flare Skirt	bronze	polished/textured	29.5"
1973	72WT	Bust Of Young Girl	chestnut	natural	
1973	72WT	Bust Of Young Girl	box elder wood		11"
1974	72WT	Bust Of Young Girl	box elder wood		11"
1974	72WT	Bust Of Young Girl	beech	natural	12"
1975	72WT	Bust Of Young Girl	oak	natural	12"
1979	72WT	Bust Of Young Girl	spltd. beech	natural	13"
1973	72BT	Flare Skirt Torso	bronze	polished	13"
1973	72BT	Flare Skirt Torso	bronze	polished	13"
1973	73BT	Flare Skirt Torso	bronze	black-green patina	12"
1976	72BT	Flare Skirt Torso	bronze	polished	12"
1976	72BT	Flare Skirt Torso	bronze	polished	13"
1976	72BT	Flare Skirt Torso	bronze	polished	13"
1976	72BT	Flare Skirt Torso	bronze	polished	12"
1976	72BT	Flare Skirt Torso	bronze	polished	13"
	72BT	Flare Skirt Torso	bronze	polished	13"
1982	72BT	Flared Skirt (small bust)	bronze	polished	10"
1984	72BT	Flared Skirt (small bust)	bronze	polished	10"

Date	Piece	Name	Material	Finish	Height
1985	72BT	Flared Skirt (small bust)	bronze	polished	11"
1985	72BT	Flared Skirt (small bust)	bronze	polished	11"
1968	73	Standing Woman	elm	polychrome	31"
1977	73W	American Woman	blk walnut	natural	33"
1969	73B	American Lady	bronze	blk patina	32"
1972	73WT	American Lady	blk walnut	natural wood	25"
1974	73WT	American Lady	beech	natural	15"
1974	73WT	American Lady	blk walnut	natural	18"
1969	73BT	American Lady	bronze	bronze patina	17"
1972	73BT	American Lady	bronze	light bronze patina	17"
1969	73BT	American Lady	bronze	light brown patina	17"
1972	73BT	American Lady	bronze	dark brown patina	17"
1977	73BT	American Lady	bronze	brown/black patina	18"
1969	74	Black Girl	walnut	polychrome	44"
1969	75	American Beauty	elm	polychrome	41"
1984	75BT	American Beauty	bronze	polished	21"
1984	75BT	American Beauty	bronze	polished	21"
1969	76	American Belle	elm	polychrome	42"
1971	77	Black Girl	blk walnut	polychrome	56"
1972	78	American Girl	elm	polychrome	17"
1972	79	Black Haired Girl	elm	polychrome	28"
1972	80	Bather	bass wood	polychrome	32"
1973	81	Beach Girl	pine	natural	28"
1973	82	Lady Sara	25-year-old chestnut		13"
1975	83	Sassafras Lady	sassafras	natural	18"
	84	Nella	chestnut	natural	
1983	84B	Nella	bronze	polished	37.5"
	84B	Nella	bronze	textured w/ dark patina	
1976	85	Walking Woman	box elder	polychrome	
1976	85B	Walking Woman	bronze	polished	
1976	85B	Walking Woman	bronze	polished	33"
1976	85B	Walking Woman	bronze	polished	33"
1977	85B	Walking Woman	bronze	polished	32"
1978	85B	Walking Woman	bronze	polished	32"
1980	85B	Walking Woman	bronze	brown patina	32"
1981	85B	Walking Woman	bronze	polished	32"
1982	85B	Walking Woman (short)	bronze	polished	31"
1984	85B	Walking Woman (larger)	bronze	polished	39"
1985	85B	Walking Woman (larger)	bronze	polished	38"
1982	85B	Reclining Woman	bronze	polished	13"
1984	85B	Reclining Woman II	bronze	polished	12"
1985	85B	Reclining Woman II	bronze	polished	12"
1986		Summertime Lady	sassafras	natural	30"
1979	86W	Summertime Lady	white oak	polychrome	48"

Date	Piece	Name	Material	Finish	Height
1978	86W	Summertime Lady	catalpa	polychrome	36"
1982	86W	Summertime Lady	spalted elm	natural	35"
1983	86W	Summertime Lady	spalted maple		37"
1979	86B	Summertime Lady	bronze	polished	29"
1980	86B	Summertime Lady	bronze	polished	
1980	86B	Summertime Lady	bronze	polished	29"
1981	86B	Summertime Lady	bronze	brown patina	29"
1982	86B	Summertime Lady	bronze	polished	28"
1982	86B	Summertime Lady	bronze	polished	28"
1985	86B	Summertime Lady	bronze	polished	28"
1985	86B	Summertime Lady	bronze	polished	28"
1981	86B	Summertime Lady (Large)	bronze	carved & polished	4.5'
1985	86B	Summertime Lady (large)	bronze	polished	50'
1982	86BT	Summertime Lady (bust)	bronze	carved & polished	30"
1985	86BT	Summertime Lady (head)	bronze	polished	17"
1984	86BT	Summertime Lady (bust)	bronze	polished	17"
1984	86BT	Summertime Lady (bust)	bronze	polished	17"
1984	86BT	Summertime Lady (bust)	bronze	polished	
1982	86BT	Summertime Lady (small bust)	bronze		12.5"
1984	86BT	Summertime Lady (small bust)	bronze	polished	12.5"
1984	86BT	Summertime Lady (small bust)	bronze	polished	12.5"
1985	86BT	Summertime Lady (head)	bronze	polished	8"
1978	86WT	Summertime Lady (long bust)	spalted beech		15"
1978	86WT	Summertime Lady (bust)	spalted maple		15"
1979	86WT	Summertime Lady (bust)	spalted beech		15"
1979	86T	Summertime Lady (bust)	spalted beech		22"
1982	86T	Summertime Lady (bust)	spalted walnut		12"
1982	86T	Summertime Lady (Missula Miss)	spalted elm	natural	10"
1984	86T	Summertime Lady (bust)	spalted maple		17"
1985	86T	Summertime Lady (bust)	spalted maple		16"
1976	87	American Woman Bust	box elder		13"
1976	88	American Woman Bust	box elder		17"
1976	89	Missoula Miss	box elder	natural	17"
1976	90	American Woman Bust	box elder	natural	14"
1978	91	Black Woman	black walnut	polychrome	45"
1977	92	American Woman	box elder	polychrome	13"
1978	92BT	American Girl (bust)	bronze	polished	12"
1979	92BT	American Girl (bust)	bronze	polished	12"
1977	92BT	American Woman (bronze bust)	bronze	polished	12"
1977	92BT	American Woman (bronze bust)	bronze	polished	12"
1978	92BT	American Woman (bronze bust)	bronze	polished	12"
1978	92BT	American Woman (bronze bust)	bronze	polished	12"
1978	92BT	American Woman (bronze bust)	bronze	polished	12"
1978	92BT	American Woman(bronze bust)	bronze	polished	12"

Date	Piece	Name	Material	Finish	Height
1982	92BT	American Woman (bronze bust)	bronze	polished	12"
1982	92BT	American Woman (bronze bust)	bronze	polished	12"
1982	92BT	American Woman (bronze bust)	bronze	polished	10"
1982	92BT	American Woman (bronze bust)	bronze	green-black patina	11"
1982	92BT	American Woman (bronze bust)	bronze	black patina	9.5"
1977	93	Woman In White (bust)	white oak	polychrome	20"
1977	94	Summertime Lady	red elm	natural	33"
1978	95	Walking Woman	white oak	polychrome	31"
1978	96	Sassafras Lady (bust)	sassafras	polychrome	22"
1978 c	96WT	Sassafras Lady (bust)	wood	polychrome	22"
1979	97	Dancing Woman	white oak	polychrome	36"
1979	97B	Dancing Woman I	bronze	polished	36"
1980	97B	Dancing Woman I	bronze	polished	36"
1982	97B	Dancing Woman I	bronze	polished	36"
1983	97B	Dancing Woman I	bronze	polished	34"
1983	97B	Dancing Woman I	bronze	polished	36"
1984	97B	Dancing Woman I	bronze	polished	36"
1984	97B	Dancing Woman I	bronze	polished	36"
1985	97B	Dancing Woman I	bronze	polished	34"
1985	97B	Dancing Woman I	bronze	polished	34"
1984	97BT	Bust of Dancing Woman I	bronze	polished	17.5"
1984	97BT	Bust of Dancing Woman I	bronze	polished	17"
1985	97BT	Bust of Dancing Woman I	bronze	polished	17"
1985	97BT	Reclining Woman (from Dancing Woman)	bronze	polished	13"
1985	97BT	Reclining Woman	bronze	polished	13"
1978	98	Girl With Hat (large bust)	catalpa wood		22"
1982	99	Young Girl (bust)	blk walnut	polychrome	16"
1976	99BT	Head of Young Girl	bronze	polished	18"
1969	99BT	Head of Young Girl	bronze	green patina	16"
1980	100	American Woman	spltd. elm	polychrome	17"
1971	101B	Love Form Head	bronze	polished	17"
1972	101B	Love Form Head	bronze	copper plated	17"
1971	101B	Love Form Head	bronze/copperplated/green		17"
1972	101B	Love Form Head	bronze/chromium-plated head		17"
1972	101B	Love Form Head	bronze	polished	18"
1978	101B	Love Form Head	bronze polished w/green patina		18"
1976	101B	Love Form Head	bronze	polished	19"
1980	101B	Love Form Head	bronze	patina	19"
1981	101B	Love Form Head	bronze	polished	19"
1981	101B	Love Form Head	bronze	polished	19"
1981	101B	Love Form Head	bronze	green patina	19"
1982	101B	Love Form Head	bronze	green/black patina	18"
1972	101B	Love Form Head	bronze	polished	8.5"
1972	101BT	Love Form Head	bronze	polished	8"

Date	Piece	Name	Material	Finish	Height
1972	101BT	Love Form Head	bronze	polished	8"
1973	101BT	Love Form Head	bronze	polished	8.5"
1974	101BT	Love Form Head	pewter	polished	8"
1975	101BT	Love Form Head	bronze	polished	7"
1975	101BT	Love Form Head	bronze	polished	7"
1975	101BT	Love Form Head	bronze	polished	7"
1976	101BT	Love Form Head	bronze	polished	7.5"
1976	101BT	Love Form Head	bronze	polished	7.5"
1976	101BT	Love Form Head	bronze	polished	7.5"
1976	101BT	Love Form Head	bronze	polished	7"
1976	101BT	Love Form Head	bronze	polished	7"
1976	101BT	Love Form Head	bronze	polished	7"
1976	101BT	Love Form Head	bronze	polished	7"
1976	101BT	Love Form Head	bronze	polished	7"
1977	101BT	Love Form Head	bronze	polished	7"
1977	101BT	Love Form Head	bronze	polished	7"
1977	101BT	Love Form Head	bronze	polished	7"
1977	101BT	Love Form Head	bronze	polished	7"
1977	101BT	Love Form Head	bronze	polished	7"
1980	101BT	Love Form Head	bronze	polished	7"
1981	101BT	Love Form Head	bronze	polished	7"
1981	101BT	Love Form Head	bronze	polished	7"
1985	101BT	Love Form Head	bronze	polished	7"
1982	101BT	Love Form Head	bronze	polished	7"
1976	101BT	Love Form Head	bronze	black patina	8"
1982	101BT	The Kiss (Double Love Form Heads)	bronze	polished	9.5"
1982	101BT	The Kiss	bronze	polished	20"
1982	101BT	The Kiss	bronze	green/black patina	21"
1982	101BT	The Kiss	bronze	polished	21"
1980	102	American Woman	catalpa	polychrome	40"
1980	103	Sensual Woman	spalted ash	natural	43"
1981	103B	Sensual Lady	bronze	polished	6'
1982	103B	Sensual Lady	bronze	polished	6'
1981	103B	Gemini	bronze	polished	6'
1984	103B	Gemini	bronze	polished	6'
1981	104	Elegant Woman	black walnut	smooth natural	6'4"
1982	104B	Elegant Woman	bronze	polished	53"
1982	104B	Elegant Woman	bronze	polished	5.5'
1982	104B	Elegant Woman	bronze	polished	5.5'
1982	104BT	Bust of Elegant Woman	bronze	patina dress	25"
1982	105	Orange Dress (Sensual Woman)	box elder	polychrome	45"
1985	105B	Sensual Woman	bronze	polished	45"
1982	106	Essence of Woman	spalted ash	polished natural	50"
1982	107	Cloche Hat Lady	oak	polychrome	22"

Date	Piece	Name	Material	Finish	Height
1982	108	Sophisticated Lady	blk walnut	natural	19"
1983	108B	Sophisticated Lady (bust)	bronze	brown patina	17"
1984	108B	Sophisticated Lady	bronze	brown patina	17"
1984	108B	Sophisticated Lady	bronze	brown patina	17"
1982	109	The American Girl	ash	polychrome	29"
1982	109B	The American Girl	bronze	polished	29"
1982	109B	The American Girl	bronze	polished	27"
1982	109B	The American Girl	bronze	polished	29"
1983	109B	The American Girl	bronze	white patina	27"
1984	109B	The American Girl	bronze	polished	27"
1985	109BT	Head of American Girl	bronze	polished	9"
1982	110	Spalted Elegant Woman	spltd. maple	natural	5'6"
1983	111	Classic Ladyspalted hop hornbeam		polished natural	36.5"
1984	111B	Classic Lady	bronze	polished	36"
1984	111B	Classic Lady	bronze	polished	36"
1983	112	Supreme Woman	walnut	smooth natural	47"
1984	112B	Supreme Woman	bronze	polished	46"
1984	113	Lady in Blue (from woman w/elbow out)	maple	polychrome	30"
1985	113BT	Flapper	bronze	polished	10.5"
1984	114	Girl With Sunhat I	spltd. maple	w/carved hair	17"
1984	114BT	Girl in Sunhat	bronze	polished	14"
1984	114BT	Girl in Sunhat	bronze	polished	14"
1984	115	Coco Bolo Lady	coco bolo	smooth oiled	21"
1984	115S	Romantic Woman	stone	White Marble	20"
1984	115B	Romantic Woman	bronze	polished	21"
1984	115B	Romantic Woman	bronze	polished	21"

Afterword

Retirement brings energy and

New Work

by Louis A. Zona,

Director: The Butler Institute of American Art

Gemini 1984.

The art of David Hostetler can be said to extend the traditions of Western sculpture, finding itself squarely within the bounds of modernist aesthetics. This said, the artist remains an anachronism. He is a classicist in an era of expressionistic eccentricities. He whittles and hand rubs, resisting a universal environment of poly-resins, laser, and the electronically generated image. He draws strength not from the toutings of Post Modernism nor from the theoretical canons of the Avant Garde, but rather from the primary life rhythms, which inspire the art of even the most primitive of cultures. John Canaday once said that Henry Moore was capable of demonstrating "the genesis of life within inanimate materials." If ever an art was inspired and conceived in direct response to natural forces, it is the sculpture of David Hostetler. Like Moore, Hostetler is one with his medium. In a sense, he recreates the material itself, continually redefining the natural in the process of defining the artistic.

The sculpture of David Hostetler is about one man's response to nature's unpredictable intensities. He explores nature's raw media, taming and calming its roughness and severity. In his hands, the wildest of wood, the coarsest of stone, and the hardest of metal are transformed to reveal their gentle sweetness, their compliant beauty. His response to nature, however, moves beyond the handling and interpretation of media. This is a man whose sensitivities to life's varied pulses affect who he is and what he does. David Hostetler comprehends with mind and senses that certain forces are well beyond man's ability to maneuver and to form (with these we are simply best to bend, being satisfied to interpret and document.) Yet, others of life's powers can be culled, manipulated, and restructured. Hostetler's success as an artist is found in the revelation that he distinguishes and moves freely between such forces. The artist has spent a lifetime knowing and unraveling nature's complexities, and like Jackson Pollock, who in responding to Hans Hofmann's advice that he simply works before nature, Hostetler too would argue that he, like Pollock, is nature.

Hostetler with *Homage to Woman*, at Wauwinet Inn on Nantucket.

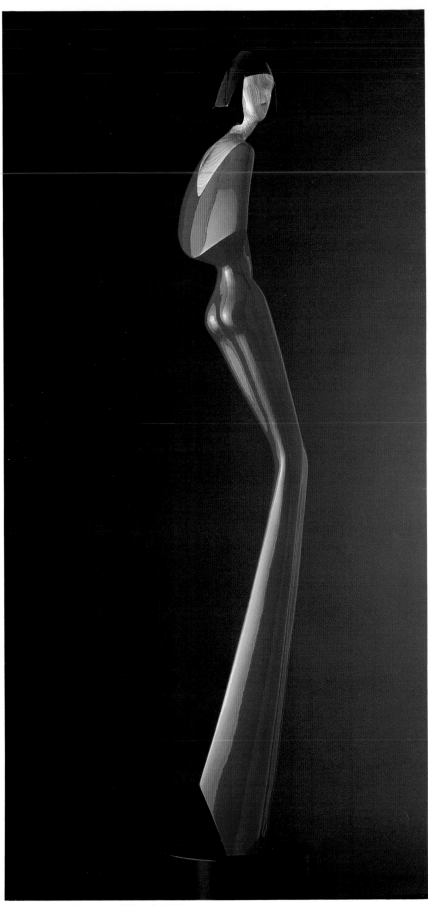

Cape Lady Painted Wood, 1986.

Even as he approaches the twenty-first century, David Hostetler remains a classicist. But his journey toward classic form is in reality a "back to the future" saga in which encounters with Myron's figurative ideals are ultimately tempered by the predictable confrontation with all that is Picasso. While it can be said that virtually anyone who today puts paint to canvas or chisel into stone is a logical descendent of Picasso, Hostetler, it could be argued, is next of kin. In both process and vision, this is so. Picasso's empathy with African craftsmen and the magic which inspired their stylized human forms parallels David Hostetler's ultrasensitivity toward primitive cultures, the drumming, the beats, the pulses which are in fact, manifested in the work. Too, the Spanish genius who gave the world cubism was ultimately responsible for the reductive process of abstraction, which would impact greatly upon the work of Constantin Brancusi and others. The simplification of involved natural forms became Brancusi's identity, and it is this purification of human form which has reached across decades to the aesthetic of David Hostetler. The surreal, morphological world of Brancusi via Picasso had more than touched the spirit of Hostetler. It in fact set into motion a universe of possibilities which would be realized when yet one more critical element was added to this inspirational equation - the schematized sculpture of Elie Nadelman.

Hostetler credits the rousing discovery of Nadelman as the key, the resolution, to what his own work would become. Nadelman, who through the refinement and reduction of human features, arrived at elegant, abstract forms that were to Hostetler a step beyond Brancusi. "I always carried Nadelman in my back pocket," he remarks, and the abridged anatomy which he observed in such Nadelman classics as *Dancer* (c. 1918) certainly led the way toward the streamlined feminine curve and counter curve forms which we have come to associate with the work of David Hostetler. It was the legendary sculptor/teacher Robert Laurent who first introduced Hostetler to Nadelman's work when the two met at Indiana University in the forties. Laurent's contribution to the artist's development also includes the fact that he was a direct carver, which seems to have nudged the Amish ancestral nerve of David Hostetler. Despite all that has been said by art scholar and critic, the artist today remains most comfortable with the label of carver. One is reminded that Alexander Calder forever discouraged the application of the term "art" to describe his creations. Art, he argued, moved the work to levels beyond the appreciation of common folk and well beyond his instinctively playful intent. David Hostetler, the carver, can recall his Pennsylvania Dutch roots and a lingering affection for American folk art. Perhaps it is the simplicity and straightforward nature of the folk idiom which early on impressed him and which touched the work. Whatever its role in the genesis of Hostetler's mature style, a regard for the informal dignity within the folk tradition would remain and continue to surface throughout his career.

The art of David Hostetler has long been identified with a singular motif, the female human form. Termed "The American Woman," the theme has evolved over a period of four decades, shifting, and changing, and adjusting in response to factors as varied as man's artistic tendencies. To trace the thematic development of "The American Woman" is to analyze the dynamics of the creative process itself. The decision to remain true to a theme is a challenge that few artists have placed upon themselves since to do so is to limit formal possibilities. The handling of weights and stresses, of line and balance, is necessarily restricted by the boundaries imposed by the theme. Although challenged

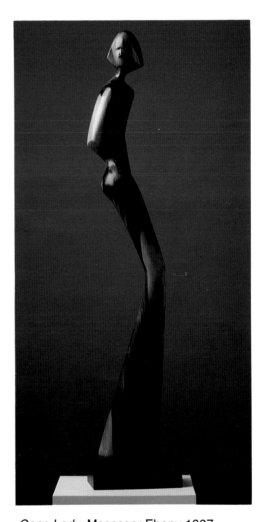

Cape Lady Macassar Ebony 1987.

Duo on the beach at Nantucket

Photographs byTerry E. Eiler

Dr. Antonia Novella watching David carve.

Examining tools with Bob Wandal at Nantucket museum.

David outside the gallery on Nantucket

Photographs by Terry E. Eiler

Susan Crehan-Hostetler at Hostetler Gallery on Nantucket

Strolling Nantucket Yacht Basin at dusk.

Homage to Woman 1991

Photographs byTerry E. Eiler

David at Bill Pew's tackle shop on Nantucket.

Surf fishing on the Nantucket's South Shore

by thematic restrictions, Hostetler's "The American Woman" series contains the spark of innovation, the wealth of diversity required to sustain it for such a long period. That diversity is readily observed through analysis of the work from a formalistic vantage point. One could objectively trace the artist's compositional solutions through years of production. Such an exercise would certainly reveal that David Hostetler has broadly applied essential formal principles. Proportion and scale, for example, in such works as *Dancing Lady* have even employed the mathematical ideal offered by the Greeks — the Golden Section. Appropriately, Hostetler the classicist, looks to the eternal notion of scientific perfection in the placement of emphases and visual divisions in this and such related works as *Dancing Woman* III. a : b = b : (a + b) and other "formulas" which have become a part of the artist's aesthetic arsenal are to David Hostetler, not the end in itself but truly the means.

Because this artist is so very capable of entertaining us with a masterful exploitation of abstract formalistic fireworks, we could be satisfied to remain at that level. But, David Hostetler is not a formalist. He is a romantic by any and every definition.

The application of a theme does indeed restrict in terms of visual articulation; but, the ongoing and focused involvement with a given subject matter provides the passion, the emotional bond which for Hostetler stands as the true substance of the work. The women of

Semaphore IV on Nantucket, 1991

David Hostetler are perhaps closer in spirit to those associated with Ziegfeld than even to those of Willem DeKooning. Despite the highly expressionistic process of DeKooning, the women on his canvas remain, after all, a structural or compositional device with passion emanating from the artist's fiery, macho application of paint and not intrinsically feminine subjects. To Hostetler, the female of the human species is indeed nature's grandest success as Milton described her "the last and best of all God's works." The "gods," as Hostetler once observed "are actually goddesses and we [men] are just tolerated." The sentiment is genuine. One need only explore the works to recognize this fact and that "The American Woman" series is in reality a love song with refrains which have spanned a career.

In 1957, the artist created *Torso*, truly the beginning of Hostetler's romantic odyssey in wood, a medium it could be argued, as inherently seductive to him as the content. This work reveals an artist who has assimilated a multiplicity of influences, most notably at this time the work of Raoul Hague. While *Torso* can be said to be a root work for reasons beyond the obvious, *American Lady* (1962) is, without doubt, seminal. The piece suggests certain stylistic directions, the mindful application of visual rudiments as well as that fascination with gesticulation of form so identifiable now as pure Hostetler. *American Lady*, which ultimately was reworked and its surface sanded smooth, is the manifestation of what would follow despite the work's rather matronly personality. A direct descendent of that pivotal piece is *American Wife* (1965), a work which expresses a sensuous charm, essentially lacking in earlier sculpture. Lean and enticingly feminine, it was truly the birth of Hostetler's Venus. It was the incantation. The sculptor had kissed his creation and the art would then breathe. David Hostetler's "The American Woman" had been born, and three decades would teach us that while we may predict certain hereditary traits, her spirit remains unpredictable. Each time she appears, it is as if the artist is at once her creator and a mere bystander who is as anxious as the rest of us to know who she is and what she is about.

At Wauwinet Inn on Nantucket, 1991.

The maturation of "The American Woman" was anything but an aging process. Hostetler imbued the series with an unmistakable girlishness, perennially fresh, continually vital. The decades which followed revealed "The American Woman" to possess a multiplicity of identities. To compare individual works of the last twenty years is to find that the artist presents the gamut of feminine temperament. *Feather Cape* is the personification of the aristocratic woman. Attired in designer wear (actually carved in the most beautiful section of Zirocote rosewood on the planet) she is decidedly an "uptown girl." She carries herself with the grace of one who has known only the finer side. In contrast *Summertime Woman* is a woman of simple elegance, refined and well bred for sure, but decidedly middle class. On the other hand, *Sensuous Woman*, of the same period, does not want us to notice her social standing or level of education. Dolled up and flirtatious, her appeal is not in the least cerebral. She is Potiphar's wife, Mata Hari and Cher rolled into one. And so it goes. David Hostetler has explored the theme of femininity with a sensitivity, a thoroughness, and a passion unparalleled in American art. Since the

IKON on Nantucket's Miacomet Beach, 1991

creation of Torso, some thirty years ago, the artist has demonstrated the effective power, the magic which narrative art can evoke through the intellect, the channeled emotions, and the hands of a master.

In 1990 Hostetler created *Ancestral Woman*. The work is a tour de force; a full step beyond the stylistic conventions established over two decades. Totemic in form, it recalls the artist's primary vernacular, his earliest ties to the primitive. But this is not entirely a cyclic move, since the piece clearly possesses the lineage of works conceived in the recent past such as *Semaphore Couple*. *Ancestral Woman's* true significance lies in the work's ability to leap back to former times while simultaneously predicting fresh

David Hostetler at Clarendon Court, Newport, Rhode Island, 1989

Photographs by Laura Elliott

channels, new thrusts. The sculpture sheds much of "The American Woman's" naturalistic leanings in favor of a universal metaphor. *Ancestral Woman* with it's narrow vertical axis, dramatically lifting an angular torso and narrowing head, seems to redefine Hostetler's intentions regarding the theme. This is the essence of woman. He has raised "The American Woman" to the realm of idol. *Ancestral Woman* stands like Athena. She is a divine personage possessed of mythical powers. The sculpture in one sense appears timeless, perhaps a product of any culture, any period in history. *Ancestral Woman* is every woman. The true impact of *Ancestral Woman* is yet to be determined. It certainly points to new territory. Like others of the artist's key works, *Ancestral Woman* introduces a new level of challenge. Each challenge of the past has been met with a range of production which has been totally accomplished — technically and conceptually. It is safe to assume that David Hostetler's audience will again be rewarded. Given the energy and gifts possessed by this artist we can assuredly count on a future rich with innovation. Sophocles once said, "One must wait until the evening before one can see how splendid the day has been." The final assessment of the sculpture of David Hostetler, the judgment of his day, promises to be splendid indeed. ●

Louis A. Zona

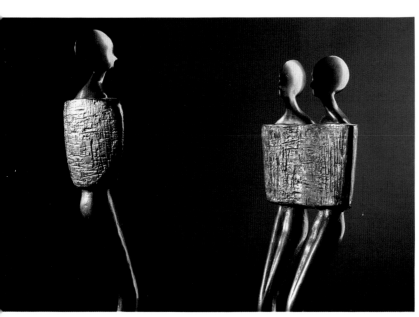

The Ritual, 1990

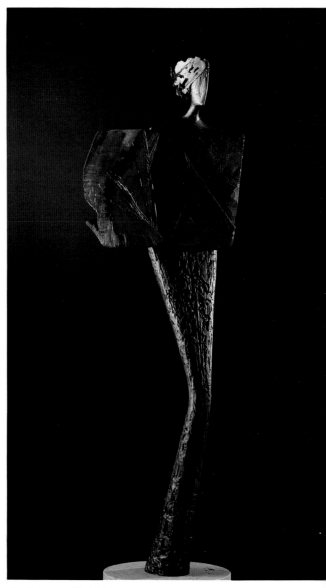

Archetype III, 1991

Photographs by Terry E. Eiler

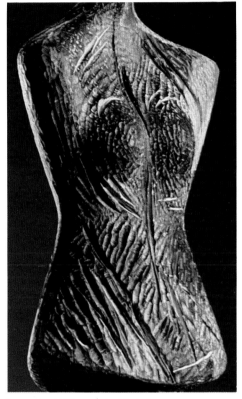

Ancestral Woman in Detail

Ancestral Woman, 1991

Date	Piece	Name	Material	Finish	Height
1985	115BT	Romantic Woman (bust)	bronze	polished	10"
1984	115 B AP 1	Romantic Woman	bronze	polished	21"
1984	115 B AP 2	Romantic Woman	bronze	polished	21"
1986	115 B 1/12	Romantic Woman	bronze	polished	21"
1986	115 S	Romantic Woman	white marble	polished	21"
1984	116 WC	Girl in White Gown	elm wood	painted	43"
1984	116 B AP 1	Girl in Long Gown	bronze		42"
1984	116 BT AP 1	Exotic Woman	bronze	patina/polished	25"
1988	116 BT AP 2	Exotic Woman	bronze	patina/polished	25"
1985	117 WC	Bust of a Young Girl	blk. walnut	painted	16"
1985	117 B	Sophisticated Lady I	bronze	patina/polished	15"
1984	118 WC	Summertime Lady	catalpa wood	smooth/natural	6' 6"
1984	118 B AP 1	Summertime Lady	bronze	black patina	6' 4"
1984	118 B AP 2	Summertime Lady	bronze	black patina	6' 4"
1985	118 B 1/5	Summertime Lady	bronze	black patina	6' 4"
1989	118 B 2/5	Summertime Lady	bronze	black patina	6' 4"
1984	119 WC	Woman in Flowing Gown	catalpa wood	painted	41"
1985	120 WC	Nantucket Woman II	red cedar	natural	16"
1985	121 WC	Woman with Long Hair	spltd. maple	smooth	18"
1985	121 B AP 1	Woman with Long Hair	bronze	polished	16.5"
1985	121 B AP 2	Woman with Long Hair	bronze	patina/polished	16.5"
1985	122	Woman in Sunhat II (bust)	catalpa wood	natural	18"
1985	122 B AP 1	Cloche Hat	bronze	texture/polished	18"
1985	122 B AP 2	Cloche Hat	bronze	texture/polished	18"
1985	123 WC	Dancing Woman II	blk. walnut	carved surface	38"
1985	124 WC	Black Beauty	blk. walnut	smooth	11.5"
1985	125 WC	Springtime Lady	blk. walnut	carved surface	43"
1985	126 BT AP 1	Bust of Springtime Lady	bronze	polished	20"
1986	126 MB AP 1	Springtime Lady Maquette	bronze	polished	12"
1987	126MB AP 2	Springtime Lady Maquette	bronze	polished	12"
1988	126MB 1/12	Springtime Lady Maquette	bronze	polished	12"
1989	126MB 2/12	Springtime Lady Maquette	bronze	polished	12"
1990	126MB 3/12	Springtime Lady Maquette	bronze	polished	12"
1991	126MB 4/12	Springtime Lady Maquette	bronze	polished	12"
1991	126MB 5/12	Springtime Lady Maquette	bronze	polished	12"
1985	126MB AP 1	Springtime Lady Maquette	bronze	green patina	12"
1986	126MB AP 2	Springtime Lady Maquette	bronze	green patina	12"
1987	126MB 1/12	Springtime Lady Maquette	bronze	green patina	12"
1985	126MB AP 1	Springtime Lady Maquette	bronze	blk. patina	12"
1988	126MB AP 1	Springtime Lady Maquette	bronze	blk. patina	12"
1987	127 MB AP	Forties Lady Maquette	bronze	brownish patina	6"
1987	127 BR AP 1	Forties Lady	bronze	polished	22"
1988	127 BR AP 2	Forties Lady	bronze	polished	22"
1989	127 BR 1/12	Forties Lady	bronze	polished	22"
1987	128 B AP	Deco Lady	bronze	polish/patina	12"

Date	Piece	Name	Material	Finish	Height
1986	129 MB AP 1	Sensous Woman	bronze	polychrome	22"
1987	129 MB AP 2	Sensous Woman	bronze	polychrome	22"
1987	129 MB 1/12	Sensous Woman	bronze	polychrome	22"
1988	129 MB 2/12	Sensous Woman	bronze	polychrome	22"
1988	129 MB 3/12	Sensous Woman	bronze	polychrome	22"
1986	130 WC	Beach Girl	catalpa wood	painted	24"
1987	131	Three Graces	bronze	polychrome	42"
1987	132 WC	Deco Lady II	catalpa wood	polychrome	16"
1987	132 B AP 1	Deco Lady II	bronze	patina/polished	14.5"
1988	133 B AP 1	Cape Lady I	bronze	polished	48"
1989	133 B AP 2	Cape Lady I	bronze	polished	48"
1987	134 WC	Cape Lady II	macassar ebony		40"
1987	135 WC	Red Cape	catalpa wood	polychrome	64"
1988	135 B AP 1	Cape Lady III	bronze	polished	64"
1988	136 MB AP 1	Dancer III Maquette	bronze	polished	18"
1988	1,36 MB AP 2	Dancer III Maquette	bronze	polished	18"
1989	136 MB 1/12	Dancer III Maquette	bronze	polished	18"
1990	136 MB 2/12	Dancer III Maquette	bronze	polished	18"
1991	136 MB 3/12	Dancer III Maquette	bronze	polished	18"
1988	137 MB AP 1	Fur Cape Maquette	bronze	patina/polished	21"
1988	137 MB AP 2	Fur Cape Maquette	bronze	patina/polished	21"
1988	138 WC	Dancer III	bocote wood	polished	35"
1989	139 WC	Fur Cape I	mahogany	polished	36"
1989	140 WC	Fur Cape II	coco bolo	polished	42"
1989	140 B AP 1	Fur Cape	bronze	patina/polished	40"
1989	141 WC	Homage to Woman I	persimmon	smooth	65"
1987	143 B AP 1	Susan-Relief	bronze	patina	27x2
1987	143 B AP 2	Susan-Relief	bronze	patina	27x2
1989	144 B AP 1	Sensous Woman	bronze	polished	47"
1990	144 F AP	Sensous Woman Fragment	bronze	patina	20"
1989	145 B AP 1	Woman Gate I	bronze	patina/polished	16.5"
1989	146 B AP 1	Woman Gate II	bronze	patina/polished	19"
1989	146 B AP 2	Woman Gate II	bronze	patina/polished	19"
1990	147 B AP 1	Woman Gate III	bronze	patina/polished	17"
1990	147 B AP 2	Woman Gate III	bronze	patina/polished	17"
	148 B	Woman Gate IV	unfinished		
	149 B	Woman Gate IV	unfinished		
1989	150 B AP 1	Semaphore	bronze	patina	40"
1989	151 B AP 1	Semaphore Woman II	bronze	patina	25"
1990	151 B AP 2	Semaphore Woman II	bronze	patina	25"
1989	152 B AP 1	Semaphore Woman III	bronze	patina	25"
1989	152 P	Semaphore Woman III	polymer	painted	25"
1989	152 P	Semaphore Woman III	polymer	painted	25"
1989	153 B AP 1	The Ritual	bronze	patina	25"
1989	154 B AP 1	Semaphore Duo	bronze	patina	26"

Date	Piece	Name	Material	Finish	Height
1990	154 B AP 2	Semaphore Duo	bronze	patina	26"
1990	154 P	Semaphore Duo	polymer	painted	27"
1990	155 B AP 1	Semaphore Woman VIII	bronze	patina	24"
1990	155 B AP 2	Semaphore Woman VIII	bronze	patina/satin	24"
1989	156 WC	Semaphore II	purpleheart wood		42"
1990	157 WC	Semaphore IV	zirocote wood	polished/textured	70"
1990	157 B AP 1	Semaphore IV	bronze	patina/satin	60"
1990	157 BB AP 1	Bust of Semaphore IV	bronze	polish/patina	18"
1989	158 WC	Cape Woman II	zirocote wood	polished	72"
1990	159 WC	Semaphore Woman IX	purpleheart wood		40"
1990	160 B AP 1	Cycladic Woman	bronze	patina	19.5"
1991	160 P	Cycladic Woman	polymer	rubbed pigment	21"
1990	161 B AP 1	Archetype I	bronze	highly textured	38"
1991	161 P	Archetype I	polymer	rubbed pigment	40"
1991	161 BW	Artifact III	bronze/purpleheart		42"
1990	162 WC	Sensous Woman II	mahogany	polished	77"
1990	163 WC	Semaphore V	purpleheart wood		40"
1991	163 B AP 1	Semaphore V	bronze	brushed/textured	41"
1990	164 WC	Semaphore X	zirocote wood	polished	63"
1990	165 WC	Ikon	elm	rough	72"
1991	166 WC	Pink Ivory Woman	pink ivory	polished/textured	23"
1991	167 WC	"Duo" Semaphore Couple	purpleheart wood		40"
1991	168 WC	Ancestral Woman	zirocote wood	textured	7.5'
1982	200 B AP 1	Eternal Woman	bronze	textured	7.5'
1989	200 B AP 2	Eternal Woman	bronze	textured	7.5'
1987	201 B AP 1	Homage to Woman	bronze	polished/textured	7'
1989	201 B AP 2	Homage to Woman	bronze	polished/textured	7'
1988	201 BT AP 1	Bust Homage to Woman	bronze	polished/textured	19"
1987	201 MB AP 1	Homage to Woman Maq	bronze	polished/textured	17.5"
1987	201 MB AP 2	Homage to Woman Maq	bronze	polished/textured	17.5"
1987	201 MB 1/12	Homage to Woman Maq	bronze	polished/textured	17.5"
1988	201 MB 2/12	Homage to Woman Maq	bronze	polished/textured	17.5"
1988	201 MB 3/12	Homage to Woman Maq	bronze	polished/textured	17.5"
1988	201 MB 4/12	Homage to Woman Maq	bronze	polished/textured	17.5"
1989	201 MB 5/12	Homage to Woman Maq	bronze	polished/textured	17.5"
1989	201 MB 6/12	Homage to Woman Maq	bronze	polished/textured	17.5"
1989	201 MB 7/12	Homage to Woman Maq	bronze	polished/textured	17.5"
1990	201 MB 8/12	Homage to Woman Maq	bronze	polished/textured	17.5"
1990	201 MB 9/12	Homage to Woman Maq	bronze	polished/textured	17.5"
1990	201 MB 10/12	Homage to Woman Maq	bronze	polished/textured	17.5"
1990	201 MB 11/12	Homage to Woman Maq	bronze	polished/textured	17.5"
1990	201 MB 12/12	Homage to Woman Maq	bronze	polished/textured	17.5"
1991	201 MP	Homage to Woman Maq	polymer	smooth/textured	12.5"

Eternal Woman 1982.

ONE–MAN EXHIBITIONS

Instituto Allendo, San Miguel de Allende, Mexico, August 1958
Massillon Museum, Massillon, Ohio, 1950, 1953, 1958, 1967, 1976, 1990
The Butler Art Institute, Youngstown, Ohio, November 1958, 1991, 1992
Ball State College, Muncie, Indiana, February 1959
Canton Art Institute, Canton, Ohio, March 1959, 1970
Avant Garde Gallery, New York, New York, April 1959
Miami Museum of Modern Art, Miami, Florida, 1959, 1962, 1969
Highland Gallery, Cincinnati, Ohio, March 1960
West Virginia Wesleyan College, Buckhannon, West Virginia, March 1960
City Club Gallery, Cleveland, Ohio, April 1960
Parkersburg Art Center, Parkersburg, West Virginia, November 1960, 1987
Schramm Galleries, Fort Lauderdale, Florida, January 1964
Loch Haven Centre, Orlando, Florida, January 1964
Sculpture Center Gallery, New York, New York, May 1965, January 1972
Gilman Galleries, Chicago, Illinois, May 1966
Little Gallery, Columbus, Ohio, April 1966, October 1967, September 1968
Ohio University Art Gallery, Athens, Ohio, 1949, 1954, 1963, 1968, 1986
Flair Gallery, Cincinnati, Ohio, June 1966
Bryson Gallery, Columbus, Ohio, September 1966
Ross Widen Gallery, Cleveland, Ohio, November 1966, 1967, 1968, 1969, 1970, 1973
Mercer University, Macon, Georgia, June 1967
Ohio Northern University, Ada, Ohio, February 1968
Harmon Gallery, Naples, Florida, March 1968
Oehlschlaeger Galleries, Sarasota, Florida, June 1968
Wisconsin State University, Oshkosh, Wisconsin, September 1968
Edna Hibel Gallery, Boston, Massachusetts, October 1968
Marietta College, Marietta, Ohio, January 1969
Kenyon College, Gambier, Ohio, January 1969
Springfield Art Association, Springfield, Ohio, February 1969
The Fort Lauderdale Museum of Arts, Fort Lauderdale, Florida, January 1969
Goshen College Art Gallery, Goshen, Indiana, April 1969
Dayton Power and Light Company, Dayton, Ohio, April 1969
Arwin Gallery, Detroit, Michigan, May 1969
Orr's Gallery, San Diego, California, August 1969

Maxwell Galleries, San Francisco, California, November 1969
The Downey Museum of Art, Downey, California, December 1969
Harriet Crane Gallery, Cincinnati, Ohio, October 1970
Huntington Galleries, Huntington, West Virginia, December 1970
Speed Museum, Louisville, Kentucky, March 1971
Ken Lloyd Associates, Lexington, Kentucky, May 1971, April 1973
Summit House, Indianapolis, Indiana, May 1971
Cultural Arts Center, Canton, Ohio, June 1971
The Mansfield Art Center, Mansfield, Ohio, February 1972
Gallery 200, Columbus, Ohio, March 1972, May 1974, 1975
James Hunt Barker Gallery, Nantucket Island, Massachusetts, July 1972, August 1973
Swearingen-Byck Gallery, Louisville, Kentucky, April 1972, March 1973
Byron Kohn Gallery, "Nantucket Junket", German Village, Columbus, Ohio,
    November 1972, 1977, 1978, 1979, 1981, 1982, 1983, 1984, 1985
Peterson Gallery, Old South Wharf, Nantucket, Massachusetts, August 1974, 1975
McCann-Wood Gallery, Lexington, Kentucky, October 1974
Strongs Gallery, Cleveland, Ohio, November 1975, 1977
Swearingen, Haynie & Helm Gallery, Louisville, Kentucky, April 1976, November 1977
Cedar Rapids Art Center, Cedar Rapids, Iowa, September 1976
Davenport Municipal Art Gallery, Davenport, Iowa, June 1976
Paine Art Center, Oshkosh, Wisconsin, October 1976
Hostetler-Mielko Gallery, Nantucket Island, Massachusetts, 1978, 1979, 1980, 1981
Nationwide Gallery, Columbus, Ohio 1981
St. Lawrence University, Richard F. Brush Gallery, Canton, New York, 1987
Judith Norman Collection, Design Center of the Americas, Dania, Florida 1987-88
Roberta Kuhn Gallery, Columbus, Ohio, 1991
Foster Harmon Gallery, Sarasota, Florida, 1991
Harmon Meeks Galleries, Naples, Florida, 1992
Kenneth Raymond Gallery, Boca Raton, Florida, 1991, 1992

PUBLIC COLLECTIONS

Canton Art Institute, Canton, Ohio
Marietta College, Marietta, Ohio
Butler Institute of American Art, Youngstown, Ohio - "Cape Woman" - bronze sculpture
Massillon Museum, Massillon, Ohio - "Yellow Hat" - wood carving
West Virginia Wesleyan University
New York State University of Fredonia, Fredonia, New York
Fort Lauderdale Museum, Fort Lauderdale, Florida
Solon Public Library, Cleveland, Ohio - "Long Haired Girl" - wood carving
Kenyon College, Gambier, Ohio
St. Lawrence University, Canton, New York - "Pony Tail" - bronze sculpture
Middle Tennessee State University, Murfreesboro, Tennessee - "American Woman" -
       wood carving
Cuyahoga Savings and Loan, One Erieview Plaze, Cleveland, Ohio - "American Queen"
       – bronze sculpture, 1969
Speed Museum, Outdoor Sculpture Garden, Louisville, Kentucky - "American Queen" -
       bronze sculpture, 1973
Milwaukee Museum, Milwaukee, Wisconsin - "Ponytail" - elmwood carving, 1974
Schumacher Collection, Capital University, Columbus, Ohio - "American Woman" - box
       elder carving, 1978
The University of Minnesota Art Gallery, Permanent Collection, Minneapolis,
       Minnesota - "American Man" - maplewood carving, 1978
The Columbus Museum of Art, Columbus, Ohio - "Standing Woman" (flare shirt) -
       bronze, 1981
Tim Horton Donut Ltd, Ontario Canada - "The Diver" - bronze, 1989
Ohio University, Athens, Ohio - "American Woman" - bronze, 1989
AHOLD. U.V., The Netherlands - "Dancer" - bocote wood, 1989
Wauwinet Inn, Nantucket, Massachusetts - "Homage to Woman" - bronze, 1987
Nestle Enterprises, Ltd., Ontario, Canada - "Committment" - bronze, 1987; "Woman
       Gate I" - bronze, 1990

Arley, Inc., Taunton, Massachusets - "Dancing Woman" - bronze, 1988

City of Reading, Pennsylvania - "Standing Woman" - bronze, 1982

T.B.I. , Inc., Manchester, New Hampshire - Woman with Long Hair - bronze, 1983

Cooper Industries, Houston, Texas - "Romantic Woman" - wood ; "American Woman" -
bronze, 1982

Mecom Companies, Houston, Texas - Sixteen bronze and wood sculptures, 1985

Museum of Fine Arts, Boston Massachusetts - "Bust of Young Girl" - black walnut
carving, 1987.

Athens Mental Health Center, Athens, Ohio - "Ritual" - bronze; "Woman Gate I" -
bronze; and "Semaphore Duo" - bronze, 1992.

GROUP EXHIBITIONS

A selected list from over two hundred group exhibitions:

Sculpture Center Gallery, New York, New York, 1956, 1965, 1966, 1970, 1971
Art U.S.A., Madison Square Garden, New York, New York, 1958
Lowe Gallery, University of Miami, Miami, Florida, 1954, 1966
The Columbus Gallery of Fine Arts, Columbus, Ohio, 1955 thru 1963
The Butler Institute of American Art, Youngstown, Ohio 1955 thru 1963, January 1970
The Ohio State Exposition, Columbus, Ohio, 1953 thru 1966
Parke-Bernet Galleries, New York, New York, 1962
Miami Museum of Modern Art, Miami, Florida, 1964-65
Ogunquit Museum of Art, Ogunquit, Maine, 1965
The Pennsylvania Academy of Fine Arts, Philadelphia, Pennsylvania, 1966
Emily Lowe Gallery, Miami, Florida, 1966
Harmon Gallery, Naples, Florida, 1967, 1968, 1970
Ashville Art Museum, Ashville, North Carolina, 1967
Oehlschlaeger Galleries, Sarasota, Florida, 1967
Oberlin College, Oberlin, Ohio, 1967
Clemson University, Clemson, South Carolina, 1967
Columbia Museum of Art, Columbia, South Carolina, 1967
Temple B'nai Abraham, New York, New York, 1967
Norton Gallery of Art, West Palm Beach, Florida, 1968
Tampa Art Institute, Tampa, Florida, 1968
Orr's Gallery, San Diego, California, November 1968
State University of New York, Oswego, New York, "The Artist-Teacher Today—USA",
    1968
The Figure International, Traveling American Fine Arts Exhibition, 1968, 1969
Centennial Art Museum, Corpus Christi,Texas, October 1968
Palomar College, San Marcos, California, November 1968

Skidmore College, Saratoga Springs, New York, December 1968
Tyler School of Fine Arts, Oswego, New York, February 1969
Tennessee Fine Arts Center, Nashville, Tennessee, May 1969
Tucson Art Center, Tucson, Arizona, September 1969
Figure in Sculpture, University of Chattanooga, Chattanooga, Tennessee, January
        1969
Smithsonian Traveling Sculpture Exhibition, 1968, 1969
Blossom Kent Invitational Outdoor Exhibition, Blossom Music Center, Kent, Ohio,
        Summer 1969
Virginia Polytechnic Invitational, Blacksburg, Virginia, February 1971
Swearingen-Byck Gallery Inaugural Exhibition, Louisville, Kentucky, April 1971
Central Ohio Artist's, The Governors Mansion, Columbus, Ohio, February 1972
Appalachian Corridors, Charleston, West Virginia, April 1972
Toledo Museum of Art Invitational, Toledo, Ohio, April 1973
Kenneth Taylor Gallery, Nantucket, Massachusetts, 1972-1982
Ann Arbor Art Association Invitational, Ann Arbor, Michigan, February 1974
American Masters Exhibition, Harmon Gallery, Naples, Florida, April 1974
Mennonite Artists Contemporary Invitational Exhibition, Goshen College, Goshen,
        Indiana, February 1975
Tatler Gallery, Hilton Head, South Carolina, May-September 1977
Columbus Museum of Fine Arts, Decorator Showcase, Columbus, Ohio, April 1977
Gallery Gemini, Palm Beach, Florida, 1977, 1978, 1982
Mennonite World Conference Exhibition, Wichita, Kansas, 1978
"Works in Wood", The Dairy Barn Southeastern Ohio Cultural Arts Center, Athens,
        Ohio, 1984, 1985
Columbus Museum of Fine Arts, "Columbus Collects", 1988
Ameriflora, Columbus, Ohio, 1992